WITHDRAWN
HARVARD LIBRARY
WITHDRAWN

The Hidden Motives of Pastoral Action

THE HIDDEN MOTIVES OF PASTORAL ACTION

Latin American Reflections

JUAN LUIS SEGUNDO, S.J.

TRANSLATED BY JOHN DRURY

ORBIS BOOKS
Maryknoll, New York 10545

The Catholic Foreign Mission Society of America (Maryknoll) recruits and trains people for overseas missionary service. Through Orbis Books Maryknoll aims to foster the international dialogue which is essential to mission. The books published, however, reflect the opinions of their authors, and are not meant to represent the official position of the Society.

First published as *Acción pastoral latinoamericana: sus motivos ocultos*, copyright © 1972 by Ediciones Búsqueda, Casilla 145, Suc. 34(B), Buenos Aires, Argentina

English translation copyright © 1978 by Orbis Books, Maryknoll, NY 10545

All rights reserved

Printed in the United States of America

Library of Congress Cataloging in Publication Data

Segundo, Juan Luis.
   The hidden motives of pastoral action.

   Translation of Acción pastoral latinoamericana.
   Includes bibliographical references.
   1. Catholic Church in Latin America. 2. Pastoral theology—Catholic Church. 3. Latin America—Social conditions—1945–   I. Title
BX 1426.2.S4313   261.8'098   77-13420
ISBN 0-88344-185-3
ISBN 0-88344-186-1 pbk.

CONTENTS

Preface to the English Translation   vii

Introduction   1

I. A Society Undergoing Great Changes   3

  Cultural Migrations   5
  The Media of Social Communication   12
  Social Awareness   18

II. A Pastoral Effort Called into Question   25

  Personal Conviction Versus
    Adherence out of Insecurity   26
  Authentic Christian Demands
    Versus Mere Protection   32
  Meaningful Community
    Versus Alliances of Convenience   37

III. Are We Trapped in a Vicious Circle?   47

  Indications of a Vicious Circle   48
  Alleged Signs of Updating   52
  A Way Out   58

IV. Difficult Transitions   65

  From Exerting Pressure to
    Nurturing Freedom   66

From Protecting Majorities to
   Fashioning Heroic Minorities   70
From Contracting Alliances to
   Relying on the Power of the Gospel   77

V.   Hidden Motives Behind the Present Pastoral Approach   83

   We Are Fearful for Ourselves   84
   We Are Fearful for the Salvation of the Masses   88
   We Are Fearful for the Gospel   92

VI.   A Different Approach   109

   Evangelization as the Primary Task   110
   Is There Evangelization in Latin America Today?   120

VII.   Elements of a Different Ecclesiology   135

Preface to the English Translation

This book reflects a dialogue that took place over a period of ten years between myself and various North Americans and Europeans who were preparing to engage in apostolic activities in Brazil. My job was to awaken in them a sound understanding of religious realities in Latin America, to keep them from imposing on Latin America the viewpoints, criteria, and guidelines that they brought with them from their own homelands.

I honestly believe that I was not very successful at that job. Paradoxically enough, the more I tried to stress certain pastoral mechanisms as being peculiar to Latin America, the more my listeners claimed that the same hidden motives were operative in the pastoral activity of the church in their own homelands—due allowance being made for differences in the socio-cultural situation. For many of my listeners, this was a real discovery, I think. It told them something, not only about their future, but also about their past.

That is why I now offer these same reflections to a human and ecclesial context different from the one envisioned at the start. Perhaps they are really more universally applicable than I had thought.

In sending these thoughts off into "exile," I had two choices open to me. One was for me to alter the socio-cultural context under discussion, to base my reflections on realities with which I am less familiar or at least make more frequent allusion to them. The other option was to leave the book as it is, urging readers to translate these remarks into a different socio-cultural context, to seek out their own examples and ponder their meaning. I opted for the latter alternative.

Introduction

Latin American pastoral activity, that is, the way in which the church carries out its function on our continent, has attracted worldwide attention for two reasons that might almost seem contradictory.

On the one hand the New World, and particularly that part of it which belongs to the Third World and is called Latin America, displays the unmistakable characteristics of a youthful church. If spiritual youthfulness and immaturity could be measured, it might even come off looking like the youngest sector of the church. It seems to be a bit indifferent to its own internal problems, as older people and institutions are not. Instead it turns its gaze outward to the surrounding reality, analyzing it, condemning it, and pledging to effect its transformation. This commitment is not viewed as a subsidiary task, as a compassionate addendum to its proper tasks of a more spiritual and religious nature. It is a commitment undertaken in the name of the church's essential task: salvation. In an even more radical and consistent way than Vatican II, it is convinced that the salvation mentioned in the gospel is the progressive, ongoing liberation of people from all the forms of enslavement that now encumber them. The Latin American church does not overlook the fact that full and complete liberation will take place outside historical time; but at the same time, with the gospel message before its eyes, it realizes that total liberation is conditional upon a liberation process in history. No magic in the hereafter will be able to make up for what human beings have failed to do here below. In this respect, then, the Latin American church comes across as a very youthful church in its radical posing of questions and its thorough involvement in the most acute problems facing our continent.

On the other hand, however, it strikes people as an exhausted and depleted church. In existence for four centuries now, it does not have enough priests of its own to carry out its functions; it must import them from abroad in such great numbers that they make up half of the priestly population. It lacks missionaries to send to its marginal inhabitants in rural regions and primitive wastes. It lacks pastoral agents of all sorts to do the work of fashioning truly liberative communities. It lacks the economic support it needs from its own faithful in order to satisfy its most urgent needs; here, once again, it must import financial aid from abroad.

What exactly is going on, then, with this church that seems at once so youthful and so decrepit? My hypothesis in these pages is scarcely original. I am not the first to point out that a certain ease in obtaining aid from abroad is helping to cover up the principal problems that should be confronted boldly by the church in Latin America. What may be of interest to the reader of these pages is the answer I offer to such questions as these: What is preventing pastoral activity in Latin America from making a fresh start? Why is that possibility passed over in silence for the most part, the implication being that mere conservation and continuity are an inescapable though perhaps desperate necessity?

It is my view that hidden motives lie behind all this silence on significant issues. Here I should like to help to dispel that paralyzing silence by attacking the hidden motives that underlie it. If these pages manage to get people talking and debating about the possibility of a more authentic and hopeful approach, they will have accomplished their purpose.

I   A Society Undergoing Great Changes

Addressing the bishops of Brazil during Vatican II, Pope Paul VI said: "You live in a country whose rate of development may well be the fastest in the world. . . . Pastoral methods must maintain a real relationship with this social change."

That comment lays the groundwork for the general problem we wish to consider here: Are pastoral methods and approaches changing at the same pace as society is? Or are they losing their effectiveness because they continue to operate in terms of a society that no longer exists?

Before we try to answer those questions, we would do well to stop for a moment and consider exactly what sort of social change is meant here. When Paul VI addressed the bishops of Brazil in 1963 and spoke about a rate of development that might well be "the fastest in the world," he could hardly have been talking about "development" or "progress" in the classic sense of the terms. Brazil displayed no such economic growth of its national product and no such social growth in the distribution of that product among various social classes. It was a few years later that Brazil would take a great economic leap forward; and even then it would not match the growth rate of the already developed countries.

Despite this fact, throughout Latin America today there is a feeling that some sort of societal change is under way, and that it is proceeding at an uncontrollable pace. The speed of this change may not have anything to do with the comparative rate in developed countries. Instead it may have to do with the feeling that it is much harder for Latin American society to absorb and assimilate the impact of this change. The change seems to outstrip our foresight and our adaptive capabilities, and so it strikes us as enormously fast. Thus the speed in question and our inability to absorb it are *cultural* in nature.

It has been rightly pointed out that Brazil not only ranges over millions of square kilometers *in space* but also stretches back over forty centuries *in time*. This is an allusion to the many different cultures that now live together in Brazil, but span a long period of time by the standards of western history. Much the same would be true of most countries in Latin America. The person born in one of our capital cities lives at the very apex of the twentieth century after Christ; the nomadic inhabitant of the Amazon may be living in a cultural world that was that of Europeans and Asians some twenty centuries before Christ.

The most important point, however, is that it is not just a matter of two different worlds living alongside each other in the same country. Internal migration within a country, and particularly migration to large urban centers, means that suddenly there is an intermingling of peoples who are culturally separated by at least twenty centuries. In other words, one of the most fantastic—and catastrophic—journeys imaginable is now in full swing on the Latin American continent. In four or five days people are making a cultural journey of five thousand years. In the space of one generation they are moving from the Egypt of the ancient pharaohs to a twentieth-century neighborhood in New York.

The migration phenomenon may be the most obvious indicator of a cultural change that is much too fast and almost humanly intolerable, but it is certainly not the only indicator. In this chapter I should like to focus on a few of the factors that are accelerating or multiplying cultural change in Latin America. Needless to say, they are not the only factors that might be mentioned. But they, along with other possible factors, pose a serious question to the church's pastoral activity. It is the question raised above: Are the church's pastoral approaches being altered and adapted at a rate in line with the speed of current cultural change?

CULTURAL MIGRATIONS

This book does not purport to offer a whole body of scientific sociological data. It merely seeks to call the reader's attention to certain factors that are intensifying and accelerating the pace of cultural change and that therefore pose a direct challenge to the pastoral activity of the church.

Starting from that basic standpoint, we are struck by the fact that statistics clearly indicate that Latin America is rapidly shifting from a predominantly rural population to a predominantly urban population. This means that the large cities in Latin America are now largely composed of human groups who left primitive rural societies only a short time ago.

Let us dwell on this point for a moment. Consider the cultural distance, often enormous, between the point of departure and the point of arrival. Consider the sudden and swift change in the lifestyle of a given individual or a given generation. Consider the large proportion of people in the cities who are affected by all that. If one does, it should be immediately evident that those people are examples of a socio-cultural phenomenon of the utmost importance. A large portion of the urban population in Latin America is suffering from what sociologists call *uprootedness.* In short, they have lost their own cultural roots and they have not found other roots to replace them.

What was the situation in the more primitive society where those people had roots? There, basically, the whole culture complex was handed down by tradition. Moreover, it was a unanimous, undisputed tradition. At first glance that might seem to be an additional factor, but in reality it is merely putting the same point another way.

The same knowledge was handed down from father to son, from remote ancestor to the youth of today. From tradition people learned how to perform a certain task, how to carry out their assigned role in society, and what their conception of the world and scale of values were to be. In a word, society worked to introduce each and every member into a plausible universe that would retain its consistency even in moments of adversity and calamity. It did this almost imperceptibly, but with the assistance of sanctions from which there ultimately was no appeal.

One can readily see that such a world can only perdure when a unanimous tradition serves as its vehicle. It simply must be isolated from other conceptions and practices that would disturb it. Outside factors would be disturbing, not necessarily because they were evil but because they would break the unified framework in which each attitude, value, and event had its own proper and plausible place. The disturbing factor is such because it punctures the unanimity of the traditional society, leaving a gaping hole in its seamless web of meanings.

To speak of an isolated society is necessarily to speak of a primitive society. To speak of unanimous societies is to speak of societies that today are considered relics of the remote past. In the more advanced countries of the western world such societies have not existed for centuries, and we could not apply that term even to their rural areas. But when we can still talk about cultural distances extending over tens of centuries in Latin America, it is obvious that the closed, unanimous, traditional society is still very much a reality here. In the course of a day or two, people in Latin America migrate from such a society to the twentieth-century societies to be found in our urban centers.

If one understands the basic mechanisms of modern urban society, one can readily imagine the impact such migration has on people, specifically in terms of *uprootedness*. What do the new arrivals know about the "culture" of the society that they must now confront? We could very well say that at the start they simply know one thing: that they must obey the orders of their employer if they want to earn enough for basic sustenance. No one bothers to tell them about urban society: What it is, how it operates, what and how it thinks. At most they will be told how to perform the job that is demanded of them.

If the cultural distance between the point of departure and the point of arrival is very great, people might spend a whole lifetime without understanding anything about their new culture except the work they are asked to perform for their pay. Such is the tragic figure Oscar Lewis found and described so vividly as the father in *The Children of Sánchez*. His migration from a traditional locality to Mexico City transformed his life into a monument to incomprehension. He did not comprehend the reason for the things that were happening to him. He did not comprehend the mechanisms and interests of his newfound society. He did not comprehend the fate of his own children. He is the very epitome of uprootedness, and yet he is only one example of what is happening to millions of Latin Americans.

Here it is worth noting one point that we shall consider more directly and extensively later on. One of the roots lost in this migration process is a certain Christian conception of life and the universe, certain values and attitudes. It was part and parcel of the person's earlier rootedness, and it is actually lost. The first thing that the newcomers to the new society learn is that their cultural roots, their certitudes, and their basic attitudes are an object of derision. What is more, they represent the most serious obstacle to their integration into their new society.

Thus it is that uprootedness leads to another sociological feature inherent in rapid cultural migrations: *insecurity*. In his *Escape From Freedom*, Erich Fromm points out the fact that even in affluent societies the phenomenon of competition generates a terrible feeling of psychic insecurity. It is often concealed or disguised, but it is very real and widespread. And that is the case when people know the rules of the game, when they are operating in a culture that is truly their own, when other features of their life are basically rooted in solid ground. What, then, will the insecurity be like when people are subjected to this same pitiless competition without knowing the rules of the game, when they possess a culture and a worldview that has nothing to do with the culture and worldview of the society on which everything now depends?

Let me offer you one single example of the problem such a person faces. From 40 to 50 percent of the Latin American population is still illiterate. Those who migrate to the big cities start out from a society where illiteracy is not experienced as a source of deep insecurity. But look at where they end up. Modern-day urban civilization is the civilization of *the document.* Everything, absolutely everything, depends on the acquisition, possession, and use of documents. Work, ownership, and everything else related to individual and family rights is under the sway of documents. It may well take great powers of imagination to feel something of the helplessness and insecurity of a person who has to confront that civilization without knowing how to read.

And to that we can add a further point. In large measure society is structured around the idea of falsifying documents and their interpretation. Moreover, the use of documents before the tribunals of justice is in fact reserved to those who can pay lawyers and court costs. Perhaps that is enough to show that there is a close relationship between illiteracy and insecurity in urban Latin America, and to indicate that millions of Latin Americans live their daily lives with hidden feelings of insecurity. And those feelings are hidden, too. For one of the minimum prerequisites for integration into urban society is to give up all external indications of any lack of self-confidence.

Given the fact of concealment, we must try to track down the traces of radical insecurity that lie buried underneath excessively positive phenomena. I am talking here about attitudes and moments in which people do seem to overcome their insecurity, but where there seems to be some disparity between the event in question and the positive feelings it evokes.

By way of example, I might point to the excessive importance that seems to be attached to relationships of kinship, neighborhood, and friendship—at least in terms of modern society. They seem to be felt as real havens of security in an otherwise chaotic and hostile world. Even more important for our consideration here are the enthusiastic crowd phenomena associated with sports events—with soccer in Latin America, for example. Instead of viewing the seemingly crazed atmosphere of a soccer match as due to the Latin temperament, we might be more on the right track if we tried to realize what those events meant for the people involved. For people who are uprooted and insecure most of the time, those sports events are almost the only moments in which they understand the rules of the game, can associate with other people and lose themselves in the crowd, and can participate in some anonymous way without being called into question or made to feel responsible for something.

Pursuing this line of thought, we might well point out that certain religious phenomena display similar features. But they are precisely the phenomena that are furthest removed from the committed personal participation that the Catholic church is now trying to inculcate.

Insecurity tends to make people more inclined to immerse themselves in some simple, impersonal emotion such as that conveyed by certain Catholic rites still in use: e.g., processions, novenas, and so forth. And when the opportunity is afforded them, they are even more inclined to seek out forms of religious community that are marked by simplicity, rhythm, and emotional enthusiasm. Thus they have recourse to pentecostal activities and syncretist rites embodying Catholic and African elements.

Before ending our discussion of this particular point, we might stress once more that the migrations of which we have been speaking are merely one of the factors now intensifying and accelerating the cultural changes that are producing so much uprootedness and insecurity. Consider, for example, the present situation of the middle class. It is the class of urban society par excellence and in affluent countries it is considered to be practically synonymous with security and immutability.

It is almost now a commonplace to say that underdeveloped countries, precisely because they are underdeveloped, tend to be rigidly divided into two and only two classes: the rich and the poor. With only rare exceptions, the big cities of Latin America are visible proof of that fact. In them we do of course find people of moderate means such as small businessmen, professionals, government workers, and specialized craftsmen. But one of the characteristics that clearly differentiates these middle-income groups from a European or North American middle class is their relative scarcity combined with their very unstable equilibrium. Any economic crisis is liable to hurl individuals and families in this group back down into the lower class, and economic crisis is endemic to countries living on the margins of the great economic empires.

This economic threat is itself a source of insecurity and uprootedness. Indeed it may be hard for us to imagine the impact of this threat on the cultural plane. The people in the middle-income groups have taken over the moral and intellectual patterns set by the upper class, and those patterns differ greatly from those of the lower class. Consider the basic intellectual attitude toward prostitution, for example. A threatened change in social class, then, would mean much more than just a reduction in income and conveniences. It would project middle-income people into a dark, unknown, and threatening world. A person living constantly on the razor's edge knows very well what that would mean and feels a radical insecurity as a result.

THE MEDIA OF SOCIAL COMMUNICATION

What we call the "media of social communication" are more properly and correctly called the "mass media" in English. They are media for communicating with large masses, or mass-directed media of communication. The injection of the term "mass" into this definition is most appropriate, for the great technological communications media of modern society are characterized by the fact that they can reach huge numbers of people.

It is obvious, for example, that "gossip" is a medium for communicating ideas and values that are circulating among the great masses of the population. But gossip does not possess the technical ability to directly affect the mass; it can only affect individuals in that mass. A street-corner conversation may reach a large number of people or a crowd. Except in rare instances, however, the number of people reached that way is miniscule when compared with the number of people who can be reached by the mass media—by television, radio, movies, and, to a lesser extent, the press.

Some people are of the opinion that the great urban centers of the present day and the mass communications media arose together by some sort of accidental convergence. In reality there was nothing accidental about it. Every large urban concentration in the modern world, even in underdeveloped countries, is a *consumer society*. And that is true even if it has many people but little to consume.

For our purposes here, then, I am going to make a distinction between "consumer society" on the one hand and "affluent society" on the other, though I am well aware of the fact that many authors use those terms synonymously. Obviously enough, mere definition does not prove anything. Its value lies in its ability to shed light on some fact or event and clearly distinguish it from some other fact or event. When some people talk about a consumer society, they mean a society whose inner motivating force seems to be the maximization of consumption—which in turn presupposes abundance or affluence as its point of departure. When I propose to use the term "consumer society" here for non-affluent societies, I am alluding to the fact that every large urban concentration becomes impossible unless it is characterized by certain features of consumption, however scarce or poorly distributed the consumer products may be.

The complicated and delicate machine that is urban society is not just directed by human beings; it also absorbs and digests human beings *as consumers*. The very subsistence of the millions who make up modern urban society depends on the creation and consumption of products that ensure survival and that can be exchanged for the satisfaction of further needs.

Obviously the products circulating in such a society cannot be of any type whatsoever. We are dealing here with the results of work efforts that are simultaneously highly specialized and unified to the maximum possible. Mass production is absolutely necessary in order to meet the needs of an urban population, and so urban populations are basically industrial. The individual artisan, who knows nothing of specialization and unification in mass terms, would quickly condemn a highly developed urban society to death. Millions of people would literally die if we were to go back to that older process of production.

To speak of an urban society is to speak of complexity and jeopardy combined to the utmost degree. Every large city is a very delicate and unstable equilibrium teetering on the brink of total ruin. It must be refashioned anew every day by people not only responding to present data but also forecasting the future. An impressive collection of specialized and complementary tasks must be carried out in a synchronized way; if they are not, the very survival of the urban population may be endangered.

Somehow we naively trust that people will continually restore this equilibrium when it has been shaken off balance, just as we trust that our internal organs will continually restore and regulate the proper level of sugar in our blood supply. We are not panicked by the thought that the regulating mechanisms might stop working. Only in rare instances, in a major blackout for example, do we glimpse the abyss that lies below our complex and ever-threatened society. And even then we are more inclined to think of *things* that must be kept in balance rather than of the countless tasks that have been entrusted to frail, unstable human beings like ourselves, tasks that we must carry out properly to keep the process going.

Take a big city like Buenos Aires, for example. It could starve to death in a few hours if even only a few of the people who work to maintain its equilibrium should suddenly decide to debate the reason for their work rather than to perform it. Yet, logically speaking, the ideological, political, social, and religious reason for their work is much more important. In the case of urban socialization and civilization, however, we all must depend on the assumption that real discussion and debate over such primordial questions is not a precondition for the actual performance of the tasks in question. The tasks simply *must* be carried out *whatever* the underlying reason for life, society, and work may be.

Urban socialization is based on the premise that the most important questions of life are to be accorded the least amount of time and space; and also that they are not just to be set aside for one's leisure time, but simply set aside, for such is their logic that even when discussed solely in one's free time they might have a determining impact on what one does during work time.

Everything I have said so far is meant to point up two new features of societal life in the great urban centers of Latin America. The first is the fact that integration into society is no longer achieved by all sharing in the same conception of the world or the same scale of values, as was the case in primitive, traditional society; integration is effected by consumption itself and its exigencies. Modern society, in other words, offers no deep cultural roots in place of those that have been lost. It unites people in the uniformity of consumption and the attitudes that will ensure such uniformity. Modern society establishes *consumer majorities,* even where scarcity prevails. For even in a situation of scarcity it is consumption itself that appears to make social integration possible.

As one can readily realize, the consumer majorities of modern society represent factors that increase people's feelings of uprootedness and insecurity. Even prolonged existence in such a society and preparation or education for integration into it root people in that society only in terms of what is most superficial. To borrow a metaphor, they join human trees at the leaves rather than at the roots.

The media of social communication depict the functional image of a society that is happy and content because it is consuming. It makes no difference whatsoever what human beings think or feel about the universe; indeed it makes no difference whether they feel anything deeply at all.

And that brings us to the second feature of societal life that is instilled and conveyed by the mass media in their service to a consumer society: i.e., the privatization and ultimately the *relativization* of all radical values and options. From everything we have considered so far, it is evident that a consumer society intimates and effectively sees to it that discussions about higher values and people's conceptions of the universe do not impede the unity and uniformity effected by the consumption process.

The most sought-after goods no longer have any connection with the maintenance of a given religion, a given worldview or ideology, or anything else of that sort. All that is necessary is that these know their place: i.e., the private sector. No one is going to ask you what your religion is as you enter the sports stadium. What is more, you are really taught not to even make mention of it if you want to make use of the goods of consumer society. The case is the same with the selling of advertised products. And it is even the same with the values conveyed unanimously by the media of social communication: respect for the police, for traffic laws, for business contracts, and so forth. None of these values are linked with a particular ideology or religion. They are values in and of themselves; every religion or worldview should pay heed to them if it wishes to live sociably and peaceably.

Sometimes the media of social communication do convey ideological elements. Now and again films, television series, and press editorials focus on themes or issues that have some connection with deeper values. But even in such cases two points must be noted. First of all, care is taken to present such themes within the limiting framework of a shared way of life that is maintained *in spite of those themes*. In other words, society and its consumption process is put above them, so that such themes and values are relativized. Second, the very presentation of widely differing values, conceptions, and religions tends to relativize them all, for they are presented in a pluralistic setting. Traditional society was based on *one single* conception of life, and that is what gave it its force and power. Modern society presents many possible conceptions as being compatible with social harmony, so long as they keep within certain limits.

In large urban centers everybody learns that nothing really important or catastrophic will occur on the social plane if a person switches from Catholicism to Protestantism, or even from liberalism to communism—so long as the switch is restricted to the private sphere. And the relativizing impact of this fact is incalculable, especially on pastoral activity. Consider what it means for any ideology or overall conception of life, be it civil or religious, that proposes to relativize consumption in the name of some higher value. Any such view will have to try to make headway against consumer society and its media of communication, especially if it not only relativizes the value of consumerism but also steps out of the purely private sphere and tries to transform the very structures of society.

We often find, for example, that a radio station is willing to give air time to the recitation of the rosary as a "private" value for some of its listeners. But if that radio station is operating in the interests of mass society and its consumerism, it will be quite hard put to transmit a Christian message with liberation content or even a free and open-ended discussion of various ideologies. A television station is much more readily inclined to broadcast a Mass than to organize a discussion among Christians as to how society might be changed.

In short, it is almost asking the impossible to expect that modern-day society should use its mass communications network as a means to transmit and inculcate any coherent or profound line of thought. For the very nature and function of those media is to serve consumer majorities rather than *ideological minorities.*

In speaking of "ideological minorities" here, I am not suggesting specific adherence to one particular set of ideas, however revolutionary they may be. I am simply suggesting that any profound idea is revolutionary to some extent insofar as a consumer society is concerned, and that it will be treated as such. Hence one can easily conclude that such an idea will not be instigated or promoted by the mass-based structures of society; it will be initiated by some minority sufficiently heroic to stand up against the prevailing flow of information and communication in society.

SOCIAL AWARENESS

As I indicated earlier, and as is evident from what we have been considering, the aforementioned phenomena in general are not peculiar to Latin America. What is peculiar to Latin America is the *rapidity of* cultural change associated with them. It is that rapidity that accounts for the radical insecurity and uprootedness felt by Latin Americans as older ideologies are replaced by consumer majorities and deep-rooted values are relativized.

If I make no attempt to focus on those particular features here, the reader should realize that these phenomena have been studied in detail by others. Migration, the structure of modern urban societies, and the mass media have come in for their share of attention; and even their connection with religious phenomena has been considered by various authors.[1] What is not treated so frequently, particularly by European and North American authors, is a third factor of change that we can call "social awareness."

The reason for this omission seems to be twofold. In its

initial stages at least, social awareness seems to be bound up with the specific character of cultural change in Latin America: i.e., with its rapidity and hence its radical impact. Moreover, in its ultimate stages this social awareness is bound up with still another factor that is peculiar to nations claiming to have a western culture, though it may be shared to some extent by other underdeveloped nations. That factor is the discovery of the wide gap between the values that are said to rule society and those interests that do in fact rule it. A more direct and open exploitation of human beings not backed up by supporting ideologies, or an affluence that would make the distorted nature of social values less evident, would undoubtedly have a far different impact on the rise of this particular factor. That is why one does not see it studied too much outside our own society in Latin America.[2]

It is difficult to determine whether social awareness is a factor intensifying cultural change or a factor tending to stabilize the situation. But while it certainly can be said that certain levels of social awareness are stabilizing, it seems undeniable that they stabilize individuals at some point far beyond their initial culture.

It is certainly a fact that traditional primitive society regards itself more as a part of nature than as the result of a voluntary, self-interested human process. In their more primitive stages, society and its roles constitute part of the natural order of things. They are no more changeable than sunrise and sunset, summer and winter. Sociologists and ethnologists have studied this particular "legitimation" of the social realm that links it with the "nature of things," "divine laws," and the order of the universe. They all seem to reach the conclusion that while this particular legitimation may have been consciously worked out and accepted by some members of such a society in the past, it is now "internalized" by all the members of the society and accepted as natural.

Now consider one of the first side-effects of migration to the city. Part of the attendant uprootedness stems from the fact that modern urban society makes it crystal-clear that there is nothing "natural" about itself, that the urban social order is a human product. Whether it be through the process of migration or the process of integration, urban consumer society assumes the task of destroying every link between social roles and natural laws. Those roles change with the consumption process, and society as a whole is a form of competition in which no one is designated for anything in particular at the outset. Everything depends on individual effort and the mechanisms people may know how to utilize.

This may well be the first spontaneous certainty that offsets the feeling of uprootedness, if one can speak of any new roots at all. In any case, from the standpoint of a new worldview, this new certainty constitutes a radical change. The only tangible value at hand, around which will cluster other values once considered more universal and loftier, is the possibility of rising in the social scale; and that is done essentially through the consumption process.

This means that more fundamental values are not just relativized so that one feels indifferent or apathetic about them; they are actually *subordinated* to the one certain value that one glimpses in an otherwise incomprehensible and threatening society. Groups that advocate values (religious groups, for example) will be accepted to the extent that their support favors that "social" evaluation of one's own individual existence or the existence of a restricted family group. The concern to get to know groups that are favorable to one's own interests and to become a part of their sphere of influence represents a cultural change of astounding rapidity; it can hardly be appreciated enough, precisely as a cultural change. A whole new scale of values is being brought into existence; in practice it has no connection with other values that we assume to be more universal and profound. To be effective, any transmission of values must take this reality into account, and the reality is all the more disconcerting when the uprootedness and insecurity are more deeply felt.

But at this point we must add a second element to this spontaneous "social" evaluation of things. It is what has been coined in Portuguese as *conscientização* ("consciousness-raising"). This element adds a critical strain to the rather ingenuous "social" evaluation that the individual assumes at the start. When they first focus on societal life, individuals tend to see anything that can be translated into increased consumption as good. They tend to believe in all the trappings and traps of paternalism, in all the societal controls that are designed to perpetuate an exploitative situation.

Even the more primitive societies of Latin America have now learned how to disguise injustice and the desire to maintain it by making some minimal concessions to greater consumption on the part of those who are most deprived. They have learned this trick from more highly developed societies. Even when consumption is not really increasing, there is an increase in the promises that consumption will increase and in the assertions that it really is increasing *overall*. Thus the interests of the exploited are naively linked up with those of their exploiters.

It is here that "conscientization" comes in. The term is rightly applied to any form of social mobilization that seeks to inculcate a more realistic and critical awareness of the real interests, particularly group interests, at work in society under the trappings of propaganda, paternalism, and promises that seek to maintain society as it is for the most part and to allow only insignificant minor social changes insofar as the total populace is concerned.

When I bring up the term "group interests," I am obviously talking about "class interests" and, in the last analysis, about the fact of class conflict. But this does not mean that conscientization is effected solely by Marxist methods. Leaving aside the whole question as to what kind of conscientization would be the most satisfactory and adequate, we must recognize that urban society in Latin America is in fact familiar with a process of conscientization that exceeds the boundaries of orthodox Marxist ideology. One brand of conscientization is inculcated in the name of the gospel message. Another brand has nationalistic overtones. Even the somewhat despised notion of "developmentalism" promotes a certain degree of conscientization in favor of social change; for it denounces as outmoded those selfish interests that are opposed to higher pay levels and a better distribution of the national income.

The point I want to bring out here is how far conscientization removes us from the oldest habit of directly evaluating cultural values. It is a gap of centuries in a real sense. Now we begin by identifying those values with the groups that have a personal interest in propagating them. Even then, our evaluation is not aimed at the group itself. We want to know the links between such and such a group and either the maintenance or the transformation of the existing social order. Only after we have verified that point, and on the basis of what we have found, will we be open to possible friendly contact with a given group and subsequent acceptance of its values.

So it is clear that conscientization takes us a long way.

Even critical conscientization, of course, represents a new rootedness in society; it is a society in which one now knows the fundamental mechanisms that guide it. At the same time, however, conscientization has put a gap of centuries between the older traditional values and our new conceptions of society and the universe. That fact should be as plain as day to anyone who looks around.

NOTES

1. See, for example, Peter Berger, *The Sacred Canopy: Elements of a Sociological Theory of Religion* (New York: Doubleday Anchor, 1969).

2. The impact of this factor, viewed from a highly conservative standpoint and in terms of the affluent nations, is presented by Arthur Kornhauser in his book, *The Politics of Mass Society* (New York: Free Press, 1959).

II A Pastoral Effort Called into Question

The previous chapter sought to prove that Pope Paul VI was not mistaken when he said that pastoral change must keep pace with the tremendous pace of cultural change in Latin America. If I dwelt on the fact of cultural change and its impact, I did so because appearances can sometimes be deceiving.

A highly accelerated rate of cultural change is certainly a fact in Latin America at present. Culturally speaking, people are crossing centuries in a matter of days or weeks. Yet this fact is often hidden under surface appearances of homogeneity and immutability. Human mimesis, the impressive surface unity produced by people's use of the same language, and the need to adapt to surrounding society and hide one's insecurity can convey the impression that today's Latin American Christians are the same as they were twenty, thirty, or even fifty years ago. They can also convey the impression that they are the same whether they live in a primitive rural society or in the hubbub of Buenos Aires or Mexico City. They may even seem to be the same because they tend to give the same old answers when they are asked why they want to baptize their children or get married "in the church."

Yet the fact is that we are confronted with radically different human beings. When and if our words, attitudes, and demands mean anything to them at all, they mean something very different from what they meant traditionally and what we would like them to mean.

In this respect the European and the North American enjoy a certain advantage. They seem to have found a key to this process of change and the new relations it entails. For them it has to do with a process of "secularization." Obviously enough, Latin America has not been immune to that process. But the change going on here, which has left traditional pastoral activity without words and without mechanisms, does not seem readily assimilable to secularization at all. We shall consider that point in greater detail later on. My point here is that the inadequacies of present pastoral methods can be very obvious even where the vast majority of the population continues to profess itself Christian and to participate in Catholic worship.

In the previous chapter we considered certain factors that are intensifying or accelerating the process of cultural change. If we now consider those factors from a slightly different standpoint, we may get some glimpse of the lack of balance existing between the rate of cultural change and the rate (or nonexistence) of pastoral change.

PERSONAL CONVICTION VERSUS ADHERENCE OUT OF INSECURITY

The generalized state of cultural uprootedness in urban society, as well as the penetration of this state into rural society through the mass media, marks the end of a social instrument that, for centuries, has performed great service for Christianity. It marks the end of *closed milieus,* or *closed societies.*

For centuries it was tradition, or traditional society, that transmitted the Christian conception of life, faith, and sacramental practice from one generation to the next. Traditional society ensured the stability of transmitted values and practically unanimous sharing of them by all. And so, precisely because this traditional society was closed to other values, creeds, and conceptions of life, the church did not need to invite each succeeding generation to accept the gospel message. With good reason the church expected that society itself would bring each succeeding generation to it.

Traditional society brought its children to baptism before they had attained the use of reason. It brought somewhat older children to the catechism. And it also exerted tremendous social pressure on people to bring adolescents and adults to the practice of the sacraments—at least several times a year and for certain events in life. It exerted the same pressure to ensure that society's public conduct would correspond with certain minimal moral standards that were compatible with Christian values. And if these were not the most radical and basic Christian values, they at least were values that were regarded as somehow in danger.

In short, then, participation in traditional society was grounded on a sharing in its declared values. It is in this precise sense, which should not be taken pejoratively here, that society constituted a closed environment; and as such it manufactured generations of Christians for centuries without the church having to worry about obtaining a *personal conviction* from the individual apart from environmental influence.

The pervasive crisis of the present day, then, has wrought a great change in this situation. It has destroyed those closed milieus. The current process of uprooting has terminated the function once exercised by the only medium in Latin America that served to transmit Christianity from one generation to the next. The closed, unanimous milieu that provided for Christian rootedness is gone.

To appreciate the dimensions of this pastoral problem, we might reflect on the example cited by one author who writes about the sociology of religion.[1] When the Curé of Ars had effected a great deal of reform in his parish, he found that one of the few public "sins" still around was dancing. His pastoral strategy went right to the root of the matter. He offered money to the only musician in town, urging him to move on to another place and provide an occasion of sin there. The musician moved on, Ars became a closed milieu, and people could no longer sin in that particular way. But if a new parish priest were to arrive in Ars today, his situation would be much more complicated even though he might find the same occasion of sin and a town that is much the same in external appearances. He might find the same sort of people, houses, and activities. But now he would find a critical difference. Each home now has its own "musician," thanks to radio, television, and hi-fi sets. Despite outward appearances, Ars is no longer a closed milieu, and its small population now lives in the cultural world of the big city. Ideas and fashions stream into it from Paris, New York, and Moscow.

To put the point another way: If an inhabitant of Ars decides not to "sin" that way today, the decision does not flow from isolation but from a personal decision and conviction. That is what is now required to overcome the occasion of sin. And if that is true in the case of moral conduct, which is a consequence of faith, it is even more true for faith itself. Faith must be brought to each individual, and each individual must personally choose it; the decision is not dictated automatically by the surrounding milieu.

If we wish to appreciate the enormity of this challenge

posed to our pastoral activity, we must take account of two facts. First, the destruction of closed milieus in Latin America has not occurred solely on the level of the village or the local social structure as a whole. It has also occurred on every level of urban society itself. It is certainly true that urban centers in Latin America have not been closed, unanimous societies for some time now. Nevertheless, the vast majority of families in the cities, backed up by the school system, did manage to maintain a closed, unanimous milieu for their children—at least until they came of age. Today the destruction of closed societies is a phenomenon apparent in family life and school life as well. Many statistical studies indicate that children and adolescents take in much more from the mass communications media than from their families or their schools. Society as a whole may still seem to be Christian, and the family and the school may even be actively such; but radio and television blandly report the seventh marriage of some well-known movie star. Day and night the mass media exert their relativizing impact on the values, attitudes, and certainties inculcated by family and school. Such is the case even if perchance the family and school do work together to inculcate unanimous values and a closed environment. Often, of course, they are in open contradiction with each other.

Thus there is much naiveté in the complaints one often hears. Parents, for example, complain that Catholic schools and colleges are not producing "convinced Christians" as they once did. Educators complain that their Catholic schools can no longer rely on the backup support once provided by a solidly Christian family. But day and night the mass media operate to relativize any such potential unanimity.

Second, we must realize that all this does not necessarily mean that people will automatically become nonbelievers. The fact is that an open society has no great difficulty in inculcating at least a *vague and nebulous adherence* to Christianity. The new uprooting does not mean that people will automatically move away from Christianity altogether. If society maintains certain vague signs of Christianity, an equally vague adherence to Christianity will be instilled in people who have no profound understanding of societal mechanisms but who readily adapt themselves to the demands of a consumer society.

Hence it is not hard to find the vast majority of people saying that they are "Christians" when they are polled on the question, just as they loyally profess their nationality when asked about it. What we must appreciate properly and fully is the difference between this "uprooted" adhesion and that inculcated by older traditional society. Along with the term "Christianity" older tradional society conveyed a unified vision of values, attitudes, and the universe. The "uprooted" adhesion to Christianity today is quite compatible with ready acceptance of a film star's seventh marriage—even when one maintains a more or less regular religious practice.

In other words, certain forms of adhesion to Christianity in the open urban society of today cannot be regarded sociologically as a guarantee that a Christian conception of life has been transmitted from one generation to the next. The milieu no longer generates or substitutes for *real personal conviction*.

This brings us to one of the most critical issues insofar as pastoral activity in Latin America is concerned. If the churches were emptying out as the process of uprooting proceeded, then our pastoral activity would have to undergo some sort of radical change in order to ensure that personal conviction would be effectively inculcated. But as we have just seen, the current uprooting does not necessarily or automatically produce a break with Christianity and its religious practices even though it does impede its transmission from one generation to the next. What is more, the curious fact is that the rapidity of this new cultural process in Latin America is retarding rather than advancing the process of secularization that should logically accompany it. The process of rapid and total uprooting produces feelings of *insecurity* that tend to make people cling desperately to those remnants of their older society that still can be found in the new urban society. That of course would include certain disparate elements of family life and, even more important for us here, certain religious rites.

Since those rites are identical with the ones they have been used to, people attend them in search of the security they have lost. These rites are innocuous from the standpoint of social integration, but they stand out clearly in a society that seems very incomprehensible and dangerous for the most part. In some direct and powerful way they seem to restore the link between uprooted people on the one hand and higher powers on the other: God, Christ, Mary, and the saints.

Right now we are not interested in exploring the motivations that are operative in this phenomenon. The point that deserves attention is the fact that the people dispensing these Christian rites must recognize what they are actually doing in their packed churches. They are dispensing security, just as the shaman or witch doctor of a primitive tribe does.[2] The comparison might well offend some people if they fail to realize the fact that the functions of a shaman should not be evaluated primarily in terms of their relationship to the "objective truth" of their conjuring. Those functions must be evaluated in terms of the indispensable social role they fulfill in a society that has no other means of escaping from the insecurity posed by a threatening universe.

The same holds true for the priests who officiate at

church rites. The "objective truth" involved is not the issue. The truth of the rite is not bound up with the question as to whether the priests or officiating persons are convinced of the meaningful content of that rite for themselves. It is bound up with the question as to whether or not the participants see the rite as somehow related effectively to the real temporal world.

The function of the shaman in a tribe is a necessary and noble one so long as primitive tribal conditions exist. It can only be discredited when new situations or possibilities alter the context. The question still to be answered, and it is a question we are not yet capable of answering in this book, is whether the church really wants to accept the shamanistic role that is being demanded of it and that it is now in fact fulfilling.

From a sociological and pastoral viewpoint, however, the more important fact is that human insecurity provides the pastoral agents of the church with a huge clientele that is capable of monopolizing all their time, strength, and energy. In the meantime, remember, Christianity is no longer being transmitted from one generation to the next by any closed milieus. A church wholly submerged in the task of providing people with security does not have the time or the personnel to fashion new methods and approaches that would replace the closed milieus of the past with a Christianity based on real personal conviction.

AUTHENTIC CHRISTIAN DEMANDS VERSUS MERE PROTECTION

If there is no personal conviction on the part of Christians, it is obvious that we cannot demand much of them. But at this point one might well ask: Why try to demand something of people that was not demanded before?

Here we would do well to recall a point that was made in the first chapter. If we want to attribute an absolute cast to some value when we live in a consumer society, and if society itself associates that value with the private sector, then we will have to fight against the consumerist current of urban society that has replaced the pressure of tradition in older closed societies. In other words, the same societal pressure that once operated in favor of the Christian conception now operates against any social incarnation of that conception. So true is this that the active presence of Christianity in the process of constructing Latin American society is wholly dependent on real personal conviction of *heroic* proportions. Only a heroic minority can present the prophetic message of God to a consumer society.

At this point one might object that we need not go so far, that Christianity can survive in the private sector that consumer society provides for deeply felt values. Christians, in other words, would not suffer any great social inconvenience if they accepted Christianity as a precondition for their own individual salvation but did not try to turn it into an instrument for liberating society as a whole.

It remains to be seen what sort of theological criteria would serve to justify such a contention. But there is no doubt that the Latin American church does in fact accept a blending of "egotistical motives" with the faith.[3] This may be due to a theology that has always viewed the matter that way, or it may be due to a heightened sense of sociological fatalism. In any case the acceptance of this intermixture can only be a temporary solution, if indeed it can be even that. If what we saw in the preceding section is true, if Christianity can no longer be transmitted without a real personal conviction, then we are faced with a very clear-cut set of alternatives: Either personal conviction is geared toward, and must result in, liberative action that runs counter to the whole conservative thrust of existing society; or else we must not only *accept* but actually cultivate egotistical motives.

Now the fact is that in modern urban society, with its pluralism and its relativization of values, we do not readily find very many egotistical motives that work in favor of Christianity. This brings us to a very critical point. Aside from not demanding anything more than the mere minimum compatible with Christianity, there is only one way of making Christianity more attractive than other styles of life and thought if we are thinking in terms of easy shortcuts rather than in terms of heroic personal conviction. That way is *to create or simply maintain consumer majorities who are artificially bound to Christianity.* That is precisely what has been done in erecting *Christian institutions.*

Let me explain this point in greater detail. If we want to spare the pastoral apparatus of the church from the effort and the danger involved in trying to inculcate in each individual a personal conviction that can stand up to social pressure, we must resort to other incentives. And the incentive that holds modern urban society together is, as we now know well, consumption. So if we can make the consumption of certain necessary items conditional upon some sort of participation in Christianity, then within the orbit of that paricular institution we will have a *consumer majority* that is Christian to some extent. The tie to Christianity is *artificial,* however, for a very simple but important reason which we shall consider shortly.

With all the formidable media at its disposal, modern society tries to make sure that the process of consumption itself is the main issue, that it is not bound up with any one value system or lifestyle. Any aspect of people's minds or hearts that might condition the process of consumption is relegated to the private sphere and relativized. Hence if we want to keep consumption and Christianity associated with each other in some way, we will have to expend enormous amounts of energy to that end. Indeed it will take an almost heroic effort. But in this case the heroism is not demanded of the individual Christian; it is demanded of the church's pastoral agents, who must now work to protect Christian individuals from the heroism that would otherwise be demanded of them.

All this may sound too vague and theoretical to some. Before proceeding, therefore, I would like to offer a few examples of the mechanism that I have just discussed in rather abstract terms.

A generalized program of instruction or education is one of the typical and necessary features of a consumer society. In older traditional society, which was structured around deeply rooted values, instruction naturally tended to be imparted *in conjunction with* those values. In a consumer society, by contrast, it is natural for that instruction to be imparted *in neutral terms* insofar as other values are concerned; for there are many different and even contradictory values around, which should not impede people's access to instruction or education itself.

Nevertheless it is possible to combat this "natural" tendency. With the support of political or economic factors, one can make the earning of a diploma conditional upon some degree of participation in the Christian way of life or catechesis. In such a setup people's concern and interest in education would produce a Christian majority. With relative ease one can use this shortcut to ensure a minimal but guaranteed participation in Christianity.

The sociological proof that such a majority has been fashioned on the basis of a consumer good rather than on the basis of Christian values is easy enough to verify. One need only offer the same catechesis and participation in Christianity *without making them a condition for the earning of a diploma.* It will soon be obvious that only a few parents and children opt for them and stick with that option.

The possibilities for using this shortcut approach are enormous and multiple. Just as people need basic instruction, so they need high school and college diplomas. They need information from the press and other media. They need political props, credit unions, labor unions, and food cooperatives. Each one of these needs can spawn a *Christian institution,* by which we mean here any institution that links Christianity with some more general civic goal or purpose.[4]

Another example will illustrate a different sort of Christian institution that is very important in pastoral terms. The laws in different countries impose negative sanctions on various forms of behavior that are considered harmful to society. Even aside from the penalty of imprisonment, access to many social goods and benefits is made conditional upon following certain patterns of conduct. For example, the situation of someone who has married a second woman while his first wife is still alive will depend on whether his country's laws permit divorce or not.

Now consider the situation in what are called "Christian" countries. For centuries their laws have operated in such a way that the goods and benefits of society would be distributed to those whose conduct is compatible with participation in the church. If we realize that fact, we can readily appreciate the extent to which the still remaining Christian majorities are rooted in that sort of civil protection. Here, too, the majority who practice a "publicly" indissoluble marriage constitute an *artificial* majority. It is not just, or not so much, that these people may actually entertain a very different conception of marriage. It is that the law itself is operating against the irreversible tendency of consumer society to privatize such values and defuse their impact on society as a whole.

Here again we find the same impact on pastoral effort. To take the burden entailed in being a heroic minority off the shoulders of the individual Christians is to transfer it to the shoulders of those engaged in pastoral work. They must struggle valiantly, desperately, and under great odds against the tendency just mentioned.

A final point is worth noting here. This effort to maintain artificial majorities under a cloak of protection instead of restricting Christianity to a heroic personal conviction shared only by a minority propels the pastoral activity of the church and its personnel outside their own proper sphere. Those segments of the church's vital forces that are not simply responding to people's demands for security are taken up with maintaining or creating Christian institutions. The survival of those institutions is such a hazardous and complicated affair that in many instances they do not even succeed in linking Christian participation with the civil objective. And even if they do manage to achieve that objective, the Christians protected by them are usually incapable of taking part in a pastoral effort designed to obtain a personal conviction from others; for these Christians themselves, stripped of their protection, possess no such conviction.

MEANINGFUL COMMUNITY VERSUS ALLIANCES OF CONVENIENCE

On the Latin American continent the church is more and more being judged by people's growing social awareness. This means that at present, and for some time to come at least, no pastoral approach can expect to keep pace with cultural changes if it fails to concern itself with *the Church's social signification as a community.*

In other words, if a person's adherence to Christianity does not stem from the motives described above (insecurity and a need for protection), then it can only stem from the conscious and deliberate acceptance of certain values. As we saw earlier, in a situation of general pervasive uprootedness the process of choosing certain values begins with *social evaluation.* One then moves on to distinguish between those groups that seek to maintain the existing social structures and those that seek to transform them so that they may benefit more people.

Thus a person's steps toward the threshold of a truly Christian conviction will not depend on an apologetics that distinguishes between the natural and the supernatural elements in the events surrounding Jesus; nor will they depend on some latent religiosity that is seeking more adequate forms of expression. The movement toward such a conviction will depend on a historical awareness which, as the gospel message describes it, is intent upon the social signs of the times and looks to them for concrete tokens of liberation.[5]

What is more, these concrete tokens of liberation are not embodied in individual persons or in ideas, but in that conjunction of both called groups. It is the social behavior of groups, within the relatively hidden mechanisms that are now being uncovered more and more, which will ultimately provide or fail to provide the threshold of attention and interest that one must cross in order to enter the realm where personal convictions come into play in modern society, and particularly in underdeveloped or exploited countries.

In any realistic pastoral effort, therefore, a decisive role will be played by the attitude and behavior of the church toward those who monopolize economic or political power for their own selfish interests. And it is not at all a matter of passing judgment on people's "intentions." In the context of our Latin American continent, any center of political or economic power that is not promoting radical reform of societal structures is working for its own selfish interests, whatever its subjective "intention" may be; and that is how it is viewed by current social awareness.

Would it be too much to say that the church, despite its commitments to liberation and with few exceptions, is actually allied with the most antipopular seats of political and economic power? Angry protest against such an assertion is justified only if one assumes that I am talking here about *subjective* complicity, that I am saying that the church is greedy for money and power and is therefore willing to subordinate its true mission to them. That is certainly not the case. But on the other hand the disclaimer in no way minimizes the fact that such alliances are an objective fact throughout the length and breadth of Latin America.

But why is that the case? It is not that the church prizes power or money in themselves. Such alliances are the logical consquence of the church's desperate attempt to maintain Christian majorities and keep them protected from themselves. In the previous section we considered what the church must do if it is seeking an easy pastoral approach and if it is not geared toward developing a heroic conviction on the part of the individual. If it wants to maintain the forms of a majority Christianity, it must resort to linking certain necessary social goods and services with some minimal degree of participation in the Christian community. The important point to be added here is that the *artificiality* of this connection has its price. The price paid by the church is a loss in its meaningfulness as a community.

Consider, for example, those countries where tradition has been very strong, and where public institutions themselves provide for the link with Christianity through public schools that are actually Catholic and laws about the indissolubility of marriage. In such countries the church needs *political* power to offset the typical tendency of modern urban society to dissociate societal goods and services needed by all from the values that individuals profess interiorly. Such political power is not in itself inherent in the church. The church is potentially capable of acquiring that power insofar as some political party or group or individual desires the church's support. They may want that support in order to take over power, or they may want it simply so that the church does not add its voice to the murmurs of discontent. But in either case Latin American politicians are well aware that the church, due to its pastoral exigencies, is extremely sensitive about the matter of state and civil institutions being associated with Christianity. Whether it is ill-advised or not, its pastoral activity is very open to the protection and ease embodied in such an arrangement. And so we find a whole range of tacit alliances, all the more widespread since the Christian beginnings of the Latin American countries still cause traces of such bartering to be preserved.

A typical example of this kind of alliance between the church and the political authorities can be found in the events that took place in Argentina when Juan Perón made his first run for election in 1945. The modern process of relativizing and privatizing values had made such headway in Argentina that in their platforms the traditional parties proposed separation of church and state, laicized public schools, and a new law permitting divorce. Perhaps Perón did not yet believe that he could win on his program for social reforms. Perhaps he wanted to make sure of his victory. Whatever the reason may have been, in his campaign he promised to maintain the Christian status quo on these issues.

For their part, the bishops of Argentina let it be known to the faithful that they should cast their vote, and that they should vote for the greater good or the lesser evil. However, there was one reservation with respect to the latter principle: They could not vote for any candidate who proposed separation of church and state, laicized schools, and a law permitting divorce.[6] Thus Christians who might be opposed or indifferent to Perón's social reforms felt compelled in conscience to vote for him because the church fixed upon the preservation of Christian privileges as an adequate and self-sufficient criterion in itself—quite independent of any judgment concerning the greater good or the lesser evil. And they were special privileges, nothing else but! When a modern and truly pluralistic country takes for granted that all its inhabitants are Catholic, what else can one call it?

And what are we to say about other situations in Latin America? Tacit and negative though it may be, is it not clearly an alliance when church authorities refuse to speak out against dictators who trample the most basic human rights under foot? Was there not an alliance with Trujillo in the Dominican Republic and Batista in Cuba, to cite two of the more glaring examples?

And yet we must make sure we interpret the problem correctly here. When we analyze these cases, we find an interesting fact to which we have already alluded and about which we shall have more to say further on. These alliances do not stem from cowardice on the part of the ecclesiastical hierarchy, from an unwillingness as individuals to face up to political authorities and their sanctions. They stem from a basic *pastoral* evaluation that does not accord as much value to the preservation of human rights as it does to the possibility of shoring up and maintaining Christian majorities with the help of the state. And that basic evaluation is *common knowledge*.

But the lessons to be learned from the Perón incident do not end with his first bid for the presidency. When he had won the support of the masses of the people, thanks to his reform program, Perón realized that he no longer had any need of an alliance with the church. So, paradoxically enough, it was he who effected separation of church and state in Argentina, laicized the public schools, and promulgated a law permitting divorce. Then most of the Argentinian bishops attacked him as a persecutor of the church, going so far as to welcome the military revolt that overthrew him. That revolt was nationalist and Catholic (in its initial phase). Once again the social changes effected during Perón's reign, for good or ill, were not taken into account at all, though they were real changes.

The example is most instructive for two basic reasons, both connected with this type of alliance between the church and the political authorities. First of all, such alliances are offered and maintained so long as no clear-cut popular support exists for the political government in question. The alliance with the church compensates for the lack or the loss of popularity. If the government does enjoy popular support, on the other hand, that support is often wielded against all ecclesiastical influence or interference or privilege. In other words, these alliances are not made with any political government, but with *non-popular* governments. And so there is a flagrant contradiction between what the church should signify socially in terms of the gospel message and what it does signify because of these alliances. That fact is not lost on the masses.

Second, the price of these alliances adds to the impact of the first factor just mentioned. Such alliances inevitably turn the church's attention away from the most glaring and fundamental human and social problems and focus it on Christian institutions. Its lack of interest in society and its structures is taken for granted, and its public declarations against injustice or for liberation are not enough to convince people otherwise.

However, there is a second possible way of maintaining these artificial and protected majorities for the church within the bosom of a consumerist society. If the government will not lend the needed support, then *money* will. If Christian institutions are not to be public institutions, then they can only exist as private and *subsidized* institutions. And here I am thinking of every kind of subsidy, because the mechanism that links the exigencies of consumption with Christianity severely limits those institutions from an economic standpoint. It shrinks the market and makes the merchandise costly. That is why the Latin American continent is a bottomless pit, as many international institutions know. Its inability to finance its own needs is chronic.

In and of itself this economic need would not be so critical. If Christians want to pay the price for such institutions, then let them. But the critical problem is the visible alliance of the church with the centers of economic power. It is particularly critical in underdeveloped and exploited countries, which end up having only two classes of people. In such countries money is not the color-blind asset and contribution of a middle class. It is the asset of those people who support the church from the proceeds of their wealth; and that wealth usually derives, directly or indirectly, from the exploitation of other human beings.

Thus, without passing judgment on individuals as such, we can say that this economic alliance has the same general signification as does the church's alliance with unpopular political governments. In order to be "the church of the poor," it must first be "the church of the rich." And that is how it is viewed by the growing social awareness of Latin Americans. It is a very concrete and tangible signification that it conveys to people. Needless to say, there are ways it can avoid hearing the judgment that people pass on it. It can stay within the narrow circle of the faithful, or it can prejudge such criticism on a priori ideological grounds.

NOTES

1. See A. Desqueyrat, *La crise religieuse des temps nouveaux* (Paris: Spes, 1955).

2. "It is impossible to overlook the way certain popular devotions are exploited for profit. . . . The gullibility of the people is exploited by religion. The promise of favors draws them in, and they find consolation in the crowd of worshippers and the illusion of a truly living faith. But it is also commercial exploitation, because their generous 'offerings' help to pay for new sanctuaries and parish churches as well as other projects. We would ask whether people might not be justified in saying that religion is the opiate of the people. In today's young people we find an attitude of disdain for all these primitive and deceitful forms of religion. If we do not take corrective measures, will there be any faith around tomorrow? . . . All this work of commercializing religion and sacramentalizing everything is possible only because 'pious' people do not know how God operates in his dealings with human beings. They do not know that God operates through secondary causes. They do not know that man is the active subject behind history, that his vocation is to subdue the material world and place it in the service of man. The only notion they have of God is that he is a fatherly God when everything goes right, and an arbitrary, vengeful God when things go wrong. We must give our people an accurate idea of how God operates. We must teach them that he is a God who respects man's freedom and dignity. Only if our Brazilian people become aware of their dignity and have enough sense to direct the course of events, will we have freed them from superstition and mumbo-jumbo. That is why the gospel is so important in freeing men from the slavery of fear, insecurity, and inferiority feelings" (Statement by three hundred Brazilian priests issued in

August 1967; Eng. trans.: "Brazilian Realities and the Church," in *Between Honesty and Hope* [Maryknoll, New York: Maryknoll Documentation Series, 1970], pp. 134–39).

3. See the document of the 1968 Medellín Conference on "Pastoral Care of the Masses," in the official English edition: *The Church in the Present-Day Transformation of Latin America in the Light of the Council* (Washington, D.C.: Latin American Division of the United States Catholic Conference, 1970), 2:119–26.

4. Here is another example. In a draft document the Latin American Conference of Christian Syndicalists (CLASC) described its own purpose and nature as follows: "CLASC is an organization for workers in rural fields and the cities. It seeks to promote, effect, and consolidate *the whole well-being of all workers* in Latin America without reservations or distinctions. *In its goals and its methods* it finds its inspiration in Christian social doctrine." Notice that civil goals associated with consumer society are linked with goals and methods (?) associated with Christian social doctrine.

5. Notice the line of argument used in a leaflet distributed by Jehovah's Witnesses: "In the light of these clear statements in the Holy Scripture, what are we to say of religious leaders who make common cause with the world, who are friends of predatory financiers and corrupt politicians, who tell people what they want to hear, curry favor, and don whatever hat seems suitable? Can such people have the right religion? And how much love do we find among the members of various popular religious organizations? Enough to make them forget racial differences? No. Enough to get them to disregard cultural and social differences? No. Enough to get them to eliminate intramural political and commercial rivalry? No. Enough to get them to overlook national differences? No. What we do get to see in time of war is Protestant killing Protestant, Catholic killing Catholic, and Jew killing Jew!"

6. See the periodical *Criterio*, Buenos Aires, November 15, 1945.

III   Are We Trapped in a Vicious Circle?

Before proceeding with our reflections here, let us draw some of the more obvious conclusions to be derived from what we have noted so far. We started out from a basic premise stipulated by Paul VI: If cultural change is proceeding at a highly accelerated pace, then pastoral change must be no less quick. After noting certain phenomena that indicate that cultural change is indeed proceeding rapidly, we were forced to conclude that pastoral activity is still using the same old methods for the most part. Those methods may have been suitable in cultures of the past, but such cultures are now disintegrating or already behind us. The surface appearances of continuity merely obscure the fact that pastoral effectiveness is a thing of the past. The methods remain the same, the results do not.

At the risk of seeming pessimistic, we must be willing to take a hard look at the overall situation just described and call it as we see it. If we do, then we are forced to conclude that pastoral activity seems to be caught in a vicious circle that becomes more and more apparent each day. And when a vicious circle is taken for granted, be it wittingly or unwittingly, it is evident that people have lost hope.

Would it be too much to say that the enormous effort

and undeniable activity of the Latin American church represents a desperate race against implacable fate on the part of its pastoral agents? If that were the case, there might be room for some hope and for new possibilities. For it is only when a situation becomes terribly desperate that people seem to undertake the reflection and decision-making required to get to the bottom of things and opt for radical alternatives, whatever the cost may be.

That brings us to a second question that is critically important in our present context: How could things have gone so far off course? If every seemingly vicious circle is really an opportunity in disguise, a chance to opt for radically new alternatives, why is it that the Latin American church always seems to opt for the traditional and dead-end alternative: for people's adhesion out of insecurity rather than out of personal conviction, for the protection of artificial majorities rather than for the inculcation of heroic Christian demands, for alliances of convenience rather than meaningful signification as a community? Why is it that the process of ecclesial updating in Latin America never seems to reach the critical threshold it should?

These are the questions we shall consider in this chapter. Our reflections here will pave the way for the thoughts to be developed in subsequent chapters.

INDICATIONS OF A VICIOUS CIRCLE

The present-day destruction of closed milieus, upon which the church once depended to transmit Christianity to each succeeding generation, confronts it with the urgent task of getting its message across to each individual person and winning a personal conviction. To the extent that this task is delayed or replaced by other tasks,

Christianity is turned into some vague sense of security and some superficial sort of adhesion. The very capacity of the church to undertake a new pastoral effort more suited to changed conditions is undermined. Though supposedly adhered to by large numbers of people, Christianity becomes so irrelevant that it cannot even recruit the personnel it needs for survival from among the native population. That is precisely the case in Latin America today.

Faced with this situation, the church is induced to attract and hold people artificially, to keep them Christian even though they may not entertain any deep personal conviction. This only intensifies its inability to face the fact that the old closed milieus are being destroyed. Two concomitant results follow: (1) Artificially protected Christians prove to be incapable of successful dialogue with non-Christians, in whom they are supposed to arouse real personal conviction for Christianity; (2) an ever increasing and disproportionate amount of pastoral effort and personnel is detoured into this work of protection and its related secular tasks.

A concrete example may help the reader to appreciate the ever increasing dimensions of this "disproportion." In the capital city of one Latin American country a study was made of the pastoral effort being undertaken at the junior high school level. The study revealed that seventy people, both priests and religious, were engaged in pedagogic, administrative, and economic tasks having to do with the education of seven hundred students in various private schools. At the same time, however, one public school with ten thousand students at the junior high school level had no priest or religious at all to care for its pastoral needs.

So we have a pastoral effort that is being restricted more and more to small groups of Christians who are protected under the wings of Christian institutions. This not only makes it more and more impossible to replace the pressure of closed milieus with a summons to personal decision-making and choice; it also systematically destroys any reasons that might prompt people to arrive at such a conviction.

As we saw in the last chapter, the tendency to make it easier for the masses to adhere to Christianity by using shortcuts inevitably leads to alliances with power centers that are regarded as against the people by current social awareness. Thus any summons designed to arouse a personal conviction about Christianity would have to operate in a context where the liberative significance of the church is quite obscure, where its alliance with conservative groups is far more obvious and taken for granted.

Where efforts are made to effect fundamental changes in the church's pastoral approach, much time has to be spent in providing excuses for the church. And since this usually means that one must distinguish between various levels and operations of the church, we end up with dichotomies. Thus, for example, a distinction is made between the church *qua* hierarchy and the church *qua* People of God. And so when people are led into ecclesial participation, their participation tends to be tense and critical, tinged with bitterness, and sometimes even marginal.

It is here that the two ends meet and we end up with an obviously vicious circle. If people are to develop a personal conviction about Christianity today, they must come to it through the workings of an active social awareness. Yet in the eyes of those who have such an awareness, the church's current pastoral effort is discredited by its alliances of convenience. On the one hand those alliances are the result of not adopting a pastoral approach designed to elicit personal conviction; on the other hand they make it all the more impossible to appeal to any such personal conviction in people.

In other words, the Latin American church is being emptied of inner substance with each succeeding generation, though this may not seem apparent in quantitative terms. There does not seem to be any possibility of adopting a new or different approach, and the old approach seems to have less and less potential. One Latin American bishop admitted that all the priests in his diocese felt they were fighting against an ineluctable process, that an air of hopelessness surrounded their efforts. Here and there, of course, we may find exceptions to that statement due to the variety of situations and the differing ability of pastoral agents to take a clear-eyed look at their situation. But the situation described by that bishop does seem to be symptomatic. Moreover, I would go so far as to say that this diagnosis is secretly shared by many who openly deny it. Seeing no solution, they feel so desperate that they can't believe things are in such a sorry state. And so the tendency is to have recourse to missionary personnel from foreign countries, using them in haphazard fashion.

Speaking for my own experience here, I would have no hesitation in saying that foreign missionaries themselves are extremely courageous and creative. I do not mean to deny the real contribution they have made, which is often far superior to that of our native personnel. The surprising and disturbing thing is that generally they are not called upon to break the existing vicious circle and initiate a new kind of pastoral approach. They are called upon to continue the old approach, which is now sapping the church of inner substance, to undertake tasks that will not produce personal conviction and native pastoral personnel.

To the extent that foreign missionaries do something different and act courageously, they deserve much credit. But the mechanism by which they are summoned to Latin America and given a pastoral task represents a tacit confession that we are faced with a hopelessly dead-end situation.

ALLEGED SIGNS OF UPDATING

Not without reason some people might regard my description of the situation above as exaggerated. So let me emphasize only one point of it here, the most crucial point: The deficiencies and flaws described above are not accidental; they are part of an obvious sociological mechanism. All the factors involved here are mutually interrelated and mutually interacting. By contrast, the reforms and other ingredients of updating that are injected into various levels of pastoral activity (nations, dioceses, or parishes) never tackle the central mechanism.

The bracing air of *aggiornamento* did not come to Latin America mainly through *Gaudium et Spes* or the overall work of Vatican II. It resulted primarily from the documents of the Medellín Conference. For various reasons, which we shall not go into here, that Conference represented the most coherent, enthusiastic, and commited meeting of Latin American bishops in recent years. The fact is that the spirit, if not the letter, of its pronouncements is clearly oriented around a pastoral effort based on personal conviction and heroic community effort to the cause of societal liberation on our continent. From its introductory message it is quite clear that the bishops meeting in Medellín had the intention of meeting the objectives proposed in their pronouncements no matter what the cost might be.

It has not been that long a period of time since the Medellín Conference, too short a time to make any overall or final judgment. Yet many priests and bishops, and the vast majority of the laity, are at one in concluding that we have stepped back from the radical tone of the Medellín pronouncements, if not from their underlying substance and reality. To some that is alarming, to some it is consoling; but all agree on the fact.

It has been said, not without reason, that it is one thing to pronounce commitments in some neutral place and something very different to commit oneself to those pronouncements where pressures, threats, and deficiencies are tangibly felt and experienced. Granting the truth in that view, I would still say that the deeper underlying reason for the current retrogression and stagnation is to be found in the *vicious circle* just described. It is a solid circle, far more solid and impenetrable than it might seem at first glance. Perhaps the bishops of Latin America decided to tackle it without realizing fully how solid it is, and its full weight only became apparent to them when they set their hands to the task.

When reforms and improvements are introduced as isolated instances, they do not improve our present pastoral effort; on the contrary, they clash with the fundamental underlying mechanisms of that effort. So our pastoral approach must be radically altered; otherwise our reforms will ultimately fall by the wayside and produce no results. A few concrete examples may help the reader to appreciate this point.

Let me cite an example that seems to be the most clear-cut and all-embracing one for our purposes here. The bishops at the Medellín Conference committed themselves to a pastoral approach centered around personal conviction. In particular they committed themselves to an approach designed to foster grassroots

Christian communities (*comunidades de base*). In contrast to a form of religious practice based on mere instinct or compulsion, the grassroots community would be composed of adults who freely reflected on their faith and drew the appropriate consequences for their individual and social life.

But there was another feature of the Medellín Conference that, at first glance, would seem to complement the emphasis on personal conviction and a related pastoral approach. The Conference stressed that reception of the sacraments should be made conditional on a real comprehension and acceptance of what they authentically signify. Thus in countless dioceses and parishes those entrusted with the task of administering baptism, first communion, and matrimony were to insist on having preliminary conversations with those who were to receive the sacraments, their parents, or their godparents.

All that seems fine. But one Latin American bishop told me that in his diocese the two pastoral exigencies just mentioned above were not only not complementary but actually contradictory in practice. And he proved his point with a wealth of statistics in black and white. If the conversations with prospective recipients of the sacraments were to be in-depth encounters regarding the faith, if they were to aid the inculcation of real personal conviction, certain obstacles would have to be overcome. And that would take a great deal of time.

Hasty talks or conversations obviously would not do when the sacraments in question had to do with important events in people's lives. Most people had some idea of the responses that the priest would want to hear, so the conversation would have to get off the beaten track and explore the real-life connections between faith and the existence of the individual. Bringing out his statistics, then, the bishop showed me that the priests in his diocese administered about a thousand baptisms a year in rural areas. If you add the celebration of Sunday Mass to that effort, you can readily see that three in-depth conversations with prospective recipients of the sacraments would probably mean that the administration of one single sacrament on the basis of personal conviction would take up the whole lifetime of a priest—allowing for postponements and other time-wasting factors. In other words, there really would be no time to devote to other sacraments of equal importance, much less time to handle the task of developing solid grassroots Christian communities.

What, then, should be done? Should priests be content to keep the conversations on a more or less formal plane? The bishop admitted that such an "improvement" would not be a decisive contribution, that it would be a waste of time for the most part. Then should priests give up the task of trying to form solid grassroots communities? If not, the work on that task could only be carried out by taking a great deal of time away from the traditional base of pastoral effort.

I have dwelt on this example to make it clear how vicious is the circle we currently face. If we want to introduce pastoral innovations and improvements, and if we do introduce them even timidly, we find that they contradict the existing pastoral approach and call for a radically different one. The new innovative measures, now regarded as necessary, seemed at first glance to complement the older approach; actually they run counter to it. Faced with that fact, the tendency is to restrict the scope and use of the innovation, or to eliminate it entirely.

Wherever we turn, we can find similar examples in critical areas of pastoral effort. An approach based on joint pastoral planning and cooperative effort proposes to develop communities engaged in serious reflection on the local and parish level. These communities supposedly would serve as the basis for new and innovative Christian communities. The assumption is that if they function aright they will be able to take over many tasks now weighing down upon priests: e.g., preparing people for the sacraments. But what do we find in fact? Such reflecting communities give rise to problems rather than solving them, unless our pastoral effort *as a whole* adopts a different approach. The reflection of lay people does not start from theology, with which the priest is familiar, but from real everyday life and its problems. And so we know only too well what will happen when a priest attends the meetings of such a group. Still performing the traditional parochial activities and knowing only that theology learned from books, he is seen more as an obstacle than as a help. He comes to offer his own contribution or to avert possible errors, but often the people in the group will eventually ask him not to bother coming to their meetings. In other words, the "improvement" envisioned here cannot be separated from the preparation of the priest himself, and that preparation will mean the alteration or curtailment of other traditional tasks. It calls the whole traditional structure of our pastoral effort into question, raising problems rather than solving them.

And what about the lay people in such groups? They are trying to reflect on the Christian message and develop a personal conviction. It is only logical that they will expect the church to show a commitment consistent with Christian principles, which would certainly include social liberation and resistance to all groups or ideologies that seek to maintain a system of exploitation and servitude.

If Christians are invited to engage in real reflection, we cannot stop them from adding two and two and coming up with the answer, though we may not allow them to have much impact on church decisions. And they will arrive at the conclusion that the church must be consistent, that it must practice what it preaches, that it must dissociate itself from all alliances and compromises with conservative, exploitative groups. Once again the seeming "improvement" threatens to unbalance the whole setup. Any improvement based on the premise of inculcating real personal conviction is, at bottom, in direct contradiction with the vicious circle based on the more traditional approach. And sooner or later this contradiction will come out into the open.

Since we have brought up the notion of a commitment to human liberation, let us consider a third example. At the Medellín Conference the bishops of Latin America labelled our socio-political situation as "institutionalized violence." They warned that it could give rise to an equally violent reaction against oppressive institutions. This warning, of course, corresponds with the feelings of many governments. They are certain that opposition groups are arming themselves secretly, and so they react with suitable methods of repression. While these methods may well match the gravity of the situation faced by the government, they are no less destructive of the most elementary human rights. Given this situation, we can readily see that the social signification of the church will depend on its taking concrete and very risky stances. Its basic and general stance on behalf of justice and freedom and the poor certainly does represent a real updating.[1] But how far will it push that commitment in countries where the fate of the masses as Christians is also bound up with its existing political ties? Here again a seeming "improvement" in pastoral practice clashes directly with the whole traditional pastoral system now in existence.

And so we find the church backing down a bit. It retreats to vague position papers in favor of justice, to vague denunciations of abstract wrongs or minor officials, and to appeals to more neutral organizations like the Vatican for strong statements. But it does not commit its pastoral system as a whole to the task, nor does it really justify the role of the church in the eyes of Christians and non-Christians who are socially aware.[2]

The aforementioned examples seem to prove that the "vicious circle" is so strong and solid a mechanism that it can absorb and ultimately devour the countless piecemeal efforts at pastoral improvement in Latin America. So these efforts cannot be adduced as proof that the situation is not as dark and gloomy as I have suggested earlier.

A WAY OUT

I have just tried to show that everything that poses as pastoral updating is really a threat to the existing pastoral approach, and that it will eventually come into open contradiction with the traditional "vicious circle." To some this might seem to be grounds for gloomy pessimism. But my feeling is exactly the opposite. If one really looks at the situation, it offers us the one hope of a way out.

We might well have reason to despair if the innovative improvements could fit into the older pastoral system without affecting or nullifying its cast as a vicious circle. But if, on the contrary, those improvements constitute a threat and outright contradiction vis-à-vis the existing system, they do so *because they really are logically part of a different overall pastoral system.* So there is no vicious circle, in the last analysis. Instead there is an alternative approach. For reasons that we shall consider in a later chapter, this alternative approach is not seen or presented or evaluated as such.

My hypothesis—and my hope—is that authentic personal conviction of a heroic sort and authentic social signification as a community constitute a *total* pastoral system for Latin America. What is more, it is a system that in all its consistency and ramifications has not been tried in Latin America, despite the fact that it seems to be the only one that can keep pace with the rapid pace of cultural change in Latin America. Precisely because it is a consistent and all-embracing option, our traditionally pastoral approach has not been successful in trying to use isolated features of that option for the sake of improving its own performance.

Here again I should like to point out that at this stage of our study we do not possess any criteria that would justify us in choosing one option over the other. When I speak about hopefulness, therefore, I do not mean to express a preference for one particular approach or system. The point I want to make here is that the vicious and closed circle of present pastoral practice does conceal the existence of two alternatives. Nothing is decided in advance. However, the fact that a sense of fatalism surrounds one of the options is symptomatic and worthy of deeper study.

At the outset we must give due place and consideration to one weighty reason that greatly helps to explain the immobility of pastoral activity in the face of rapid cultural changes. As we shall see, this historical reason is intimately bound up with the vicious circle we have been considering; and it also reveals to what extent a change of pastoral orientation in Latin America will represent an awesome new beginning rather than a mere supplementary step.

To explore this historical reason, we must go back to the social facts that were briefly pointed out in Chapter I. There we noted that the feeling of uprootedness, the tendencies to relativize and privatize values in consumer society, and the contemporary growth of social awareness were worldwide factors, not factors peculiar to Latin America. What is peculiar to Latin America is the rapid pace at which these changes are taking place on the cultural scene. Comparing the starting point with the finishing point, we can say that the cultural change in Latin America would have been far greater and faster than in Europe even if it had taken place over the same basic period of time. Hence the feelings of uprootedness are far more intense in Latin America. But the mass exodus to the cities is a very recent phenomenon in Latin America. Such industrialization is a recent arrival here, *a single generation* of pastoral workers has witnessed cultural dislocations that extended over a period of two centuries in Europe.

The same could be said of the other factors intensifying or accelerating cultural change. Their impact has been awesome and of very recent vintage. They can be measured in terms of a few years, and they have occurred in the space of one generation. This means we are faced with a fact of tremendous importance: Most Latin American bishops over sixty years of age today began their ministry in one kind of society; now they are finishing their lives as directors of pastoral activity in a very different sort of society. What is more, the church that should have undergone a similar change was a church *very poor in human resources* for any such change. This second point reinforces the first, and it brings us to the explanation we had been seeking.

By the very fact that the Latin American church was a transplanted colonial church, it has always been poor in human personnel. The church here was not transmitted through the existing human culture, as it was in Europe; it was transmitted through the culture of the *conquistadores*. To be sure, the fusion of the two was often so great that the native cultures and religions disappeared insofar as anyone could see. Nevertheless, outside the middle classes, which have been European to a greater or lesser extent, the Christianity lived on this continent has been cast in a foreign, alien mold. This is particularly true insofar as its basic representative, the priest, has been concerned. Either the priests have continued to be Europeans, or else they have been Europeanized by the long years of training in seminaries based on European models.

The end result has been a great deal of clericalism. On the one hand the priest exercised indisputable authority and domination because he lived in the culture of the masters and enjoyed sacred powers. On the other hand there was a great deal of passivity because a great religious and cultural vacuum existed between the responsible officials of the church and its clients.

Putting all these facts together, we can see the critical nature of the situation. At a time when society is changing at a dizzying rate of speed and the church should match that pace of change, it has only a very small number of people who are really interested in building up the church. Quite aside from the fact that resistance to change is logically found in any group of people, any important change in the church's pastoral effort would presuppose the mobilization of the laity. But a laity capable of being mobilized for the task has not existed, except for some members of the urban middle class.

Thus the underlying reasons for the vicious circle were

already present when the change came. We may maintain that every crisis is an opportunity, that we are not caught in a vicious circle but open to an alternative approach. But when we realize that choosing an alternative approach means that the church would have to start all over insofar as 95 percent of the Latin American population is concerned, we can readily undertand why it might see the situation as a race against doom rather than an opportunity to adopt a different course.

But even granting the validity of this initial explanation, we are still left with certain interesting questions: Why, for the most part, hasn't the second alternative been treated as such? Why do people only consider certain elements of that alternative option as isolated phenomena, presuming that the existing approach should basically be maintained?

My feeling is that in exploring these questions we will be able to get down to the real but hidden motives underlying the present pastoral approach in Latin America.

NOTES

1. See, for example, the message by eighteen bishops of the Third World. It has this to say, among other things: "Taking account of the necessary preconditions for material progress in some areas, the Church in the last hundred years has tolerated capitalism, its loans at a legitimate interest rate, and its other mechanisms that are hardly in conformity with the moral code of the prophets and the gospel. But she cannot help but rejoice over the appearance of another social system that is less at variance with this moral code. Tomorrow's Christians must follow the lead of Paul VI, retracing the Christian roots that lie behind the moral values of solidarity and fraternity (cf. *Ecclesiam suam*). Christians must show that 'authentic socialism is Christianity lived to the full, in basic equality and with a fair distribution of goods.' Instead of opposing it, we must learn to accept joyfully a form of societal life that is better adapted to our times and more in tune with the spirit of the gospel" ("A Letter to the Peoples of the Third World," in *Between Honesty and Hope* [Maryknoll, New York: Maryknoll Documentation Series, 1970] pp. 3–12).

2. It is well to remember that we still find curious episcopal statements such as the following in certain recent works: "The landlord and landowner have a great role to play. . . . The dress of their families and themselves should be respectable and modest. They should do what they can to regularize illegitimate unions. They should curb alcoholism and gambling, fostering good types of entertainment and diversion. They should consecrate their hearth and agricultural produce to the Sacred Heart of Jesus and the Immaculate Heart of Mary, inviting their workers to do the same in their respective homes. . . . In this way let the proprietary farmer work and fight vigorously to defend what is his, . . . doing that out of love for justice and Christian civilization" (In *Reforma agraria questão de consciencia* [São Paulo: Ed. Vera Cruz, 1961]).

IV   Difficult Transitions

The last chapter differed from the first two chapters in that it depicted a general panorama and formulated a hypothesis rather than ascertaining facts. Now one's acceptance of a panorama and one's sympathy with a hypothesis depend a great deal on one's temperament, angle of vision, and pastoral specialization. For that reason I did not expect to do anything more in the last chapter than establish a bridge or connecting link between the *facts* narrated in the first two chapters and the *facts* that will be presented in this and the following two chapters.

Let us assume for the moment that the vicious circle examined earlier represents nothing more than the rejection of another option that is at least theoretically possible. Let us further assume that the choice of the alternative option would come down to starting over from scratch. We might then pose a question that might seem to be rather naive: What overwhelming difficulty prevents us from choosing the alternative option?

Ingenuous as that question may be, it has merit and pertinence because it would force people to spell out the reasons that tacitly underlie their usual responses justifying the present pastoral approach as the obvious and only sensible one.

In this chapter, then, we shall consider what it would mean in practice if we were to focus pastoral activity in

Latin America around real personal conviction backed up by ecclesial signification as a community.

FROM EXERTING PRESSURE TO NURTURING FREEDOM

As even the most cursory logical consideration shows, and as Vatican II proclaimed in its documents, real personal conviction can mature only in an atmosphere of liberty. Any pressure exerted on an adult will situate the resulting conviction on a very superficial level, where it will be at the mercy of every form of counterpressure as well as any effective elimination of the original pressure exerted.

Now the older pastoral approach based on closed milieus was an approach based on pressure. So is the more recent approach that has replaced the old order of Christendom with artificial consumer majorities. This means that the church is used to speaking in a context where it exerts pressure, and that it finds itself quite defenseless when there is no possibility of controlling its audience in some way.

Two examples will make this point clearer. The first has to do with a now classic institution: the Catholic university. In a certain Latin American country the former provincial of the Jesuits decided that it was the right moment to create such a university. The existing state university was a lay institution, and hence it did not permit any sort of pastoral work within its confines. However, the father general of the Jesuits replied that the time did not seem right to found a Catholic university. As a preliminary step in that direction, he suggested that the Jesuits dedicate themselves to a pastoral effort among the students of the existing university. At a meeting to discuss the matter further the former provincial, now a bishop, disagreed with the father general. To prove his point, he appealed to his own experience. He had found that whenever he tried to talk about the Christian message to a university student, the student simply had shown no interest in listening to him. In a Catholic university, the students would be forced to sit there and listen to that message. It was the only way to get something to them that they would not listen to of their own free will.

Rarely does one get such clear-cut and frank testimony of the difficulty faced by any pastoral effort that addresses itself to an audience that is not being pressured. Pastoral workers will not often say explicitly that people are not interested in what they have to say, that they walk away and won't listen. But that is the feeling that lies buried in the minds and hearts of most pastoral agents, especially priests and others who have a more codified and stereotyped message to offer.

The second example reveals the same thing in a different context. It has to do with the aid that the hierarchical church offers to the poor. Although this example is not from Latin America, the problem surrounding it is very much bound up with the situation as we described it in the first chapter. A priest from the diocese of Brooklyn explained to me that the greatest crisis in his life occurred when he was transferred from a predominantly Puerto Rican parish to a typical middle-class parish. In the former parish, he said, "I was almost like the fourth person of the Trinity. They were willing to listen to me talk for hours. They needed me for everything, at every level of life: for housing, jobs, civil rights, documents, and so forth. When I went to the middle-class parish, I found that no one needed me for any of those things. As a result, they were not inclined to listen to me talk, except for the sermon at Sunday Mass."

This second example adds something to the first. It shows that church pressure continues to exist even outside the boundaries of more formal institutions. What is more, the priest is used to exercising such pressure. He takes that for granted until something happens to reveal the real reason for people's acceptance of him and the pressure he exercises. The reference to the middle-class parish also brings out another form of pressure that is more disguised. In that parish people do listen to the sermon at Sunday Mass, but we should have no illusions about that fact. Their behavior does not indicate any willingness or deliberate interest. Even in the ranks of the middle class, and even more so in the ranks of the uprooted, the Mass has a tranquilizing effect; it makes people feel that they are on the right side of God. But that, too, is an important and serious form of pressure.

If my statement seems exaggerated, one can always try an experiment. Let the precept of attending Mass be fulfilled without including a sermon in the Mass itself. Then invite people to come back later in the day, if they wish, to hear a sermon in the church or someplace else. The number of those missing, especially after the initial curiosity has worn off, should be a good indication of the number of people who hear Mass out of pressure.

Why is it that a Sister of Charity can talk about Christianity in a hospital but not with equal effect in a factory or on a street corner? The answer is easy enough to find. The sick patient cannot take off at will if he is bored by what the nun is saying. He cannot offend her either, because he is directly or indirectly dependent on her for many of the hospital services he receives. And if he is seriously ill, he is also afraid.

So difficult and so obvious is the pastoral transition from use of pressure to reliance on personal freedom that more than one observer gets the same impression about the pastoral effort of the church in Latin America. It is clearly a pastoral effort aimed primarily at children, sick people, and the dying—which is to say, at people whose ability to freely walk away from the message is seriously diminished.

In this connection we do well to note that the theology handed down to the priest has had a lot to do with this pastoral situation. Theology presented certain matters as important in themselves. And since society exerted pressure on people in the church's favor, the priest expected that people would automatically develop a real interest in these "important" matters. That expectation would have been absurd if it had not been backed up by societal pressure, some of its institutions, and the feelings of insecurity that found expression in certain religious forms.

The last mentioned factor offers us numerous examples of a pastoral effort based on pressure. At present in Latin America we find numerous pastoral rites centered around shrines and the dead. There is rather general agreement that most of these rites and activities are deviant forms of religiosity that often have nothing at all to do with Christ. This is particularly true of the shrine devotions with their attendant pilgrimages, vigils, devotions, legends, miracles, promises, and donations. But they are used as a *base* for pastoral activity because they attract people, because they serve as a springboard for getting people to listen to the teaching of the church. Of course it is true that the explicit intention of the church is to correct the deviations that are found in such rites and devotions. But no matter how determined that intention is, the fact remains that our pastoral approach instinctively looks for situations in which it will have a captive audience.

Even the conversations or meetings held prior to the

reception of the sacraments represent another example of the same tendency. They provide another opportunity for the priest or pastoral agent to get a captive audience. Indeed that is the basic presupposition that underlies them. For if the presupposition was that those seeking the sacraments were aware of what they were doing, or if it was that people would not seek the sacraments if they were not aware of what they were doing, then such a pastoral approach would have no purpose. It makes sense only on the supposition that even though people may not have any real personal conviction, the obligatoriness of the sacrament pressures people into listening to the preliminary talks even if they are not really interested.

The reader should realize here that these remarks are not meant as a criticism. As I indicated earlier, no such criticism is yet possible since we have not formulated the basic criteria for such criticism. The point of my remarks is to show that if the church wants to have a pastoral approach based on personal conviction, then it must go against all its customary habits and structures and start by leaving its adult interlocutor free and unpressured. This will mean it must risk twenty failures or more to achieve one success. Of course no one can estimate the exact ratio here, but I hazard a figure to show what a different approach would entail.

FROM PROTECTING MAJORITIES TO FASHIONING HEROIC MINORITIES

Leaving aside the fact that a personal conviction could hardly be called orthodox or Christian if it did not espouse social liberation, we can readily see that Christians must be a minority if they actually fight against the process of relativization that is inherent in a consumer society. While that minority might not be as small as some fear, it still would run counter to the majority thrust of society as a whole.

The reality of that fact is not easy to accept when one has lived in a majority situation that seemed solid and easy to manage insofar as the church is concerned.

I say "seemed" here because the historical situation is clear enough. For some time now it has been obvious that Christians willing to turn the Christian message into action constituted a small minority in Latin America. Hurtado's book, *¿Es Chile un país católico?* raised a stir before Godin came out with his book, *France, pays de mission?* The latter became more famous because it was published in Europe.

Take the case of Mexico, for example. For more than fifty years it has been governed by a clique which is one of the most antireligious in our hemisphere—with the exception of Cuba today. Yet the overwhelming majority of its people are Catholics. In the face of that fact must we not ask ourselves where the real Christians of Mexico are to be found insofar as action is concerned? Are they not to be found in the very small minority who have some say in running Mexico's affairs of state?[1]

It is clear, at any rate, that there are two different ways to count Christian heads. One is the statistical approach based on minimal requirements: baptism, some practice of the sacraments, profession of adherence to Christianity in censuses, and the absence of heresies as defined in Denzinger. The second way of counting Christians only considers those who are willing to carry the Christian message to the rest of society, to tolerate contact with other ideas and conceptions of life and win out over them, and to commit themselves personally to a radical transformation of society in line with Christ's message.

The first approach certainly gives us Christian majorities of up to 90 percent. But they are insecure majorities, and we have already considered the price that the church must pay to get them. The second approach requires a coherent practice of Christianity as its base. Even attendance at Sunday Mass is not an adequate criterion in this case, and we know that in the big cities such attendance runs about 10 percent.

The difficulty in making the pastoral transition under consideration here is not a matter of acknowledging the two different statistical yardsticks. It is in basing our pastoral approach on the second yardstick, with all the shocks that may entail.

A poll in one city indicated that people would attend Sunday Mass if the site of worship averaged no more than four hundred meters from their home. The instructive pastoral reaction, which is typical of Latin America, was to build houses of worship within that limit. But what are we to make of Christians who are not inclined to follow their faith if it forces them to walk more than eight hundred meters on a Sunday? What are we to do with such Christians? No thought at all was given to such questions.

The general rule of pastoral prudence can be summed up in these words: *the absolute minimum in obligations in order to keep the maximum number of people.* Needless to say, no one envisions reducing that minimum below the level set by faith and canon law. No one envisions getting rid of the Sunday Mass obligation or the indissolubility of marriage. But assuming that this minimum has been determined and fixed, one would say that it was pastoral imprudence to add further obligations that would alienate many people. Of course this minimum would include those Christian institutions that keep Christianity protected in artificial Christian majorities instead of obliging people to carry that message to the rest of society.

A contrary example, quite unique in this area, may help us to appreciate the general norm and its underpinnings. It may also help us to see how difficult it is for pastoral practice to shift from the protection of artificial majorities to the formation of heroic minorities. The case in question covers a long time span and a complicated state of affairs, so I shall merely summarize the high points.

The scene of this particular set of events was the diocese of Gonaives in Haiti. One of the pastoral problems typical of Latin American areas where there is a large black population is that of Afro-Christian syncretism. In such areas we find an almost inextricable mixture of elements from African tradition on the one hand and Christianity on the other. Beliefs, ceremonies, and personalities from both strains meet and merge. To fully appreciate the problem, the reader must realize that the problem goes back decades and even centuries and that it can be found, with local variations, wherever there is a strong native tradition from the past. Wherever we find strong African or native Indian traditions, Christianity stands over against a resurgence of native religious elements. And sometimes those elements are enshrined in Christian forms.[2]

In passing, we might note the problem this poses for a pastoral effort that seeks to hold a maximum number of Christians by imposing a minimum number of obligations. Faced with the fact of syncretism, how are we to tell whether the minimum has been met or not? Obviously we are dealing with heterodoxy when Christian figures such as Jesus and Mary are equated with African gods and goddesses. But on the whole pastoral directors are reluctant to plunge into a problem whose solution seems difficult, if not impossible.

Bishop Robert of Gonaives, however, chose to face the issue. At first he adopted the usual approach, warning Christians that the two sets of beliefs were quite different and even incompatible. This warning has never had much impact on syncretist minds, however, because in their view the Catholic priest simply has to say such things. That is his role in the context, and everybody calmly accepts that and carries on with the syncretist ways.

Realizing that his warnings were in vain, Bishop Robert decided to tackle the problem at its roots. Fully realizing that he would be able to count on only a small minority of Christians at best, he closed his churches to all those who refused to abandon African beliefs and practices; he also refused to administer the sacraments to them. How he did this in practice is not important here. The point is that his Christian flock was reduced to a minority amounting to no more than 10 percent of the population. That population had always been considered almost 100 percent Christian.

It would be a mistake, however, to assume that Bishop Robert chose this minority *over against* the majority. To those who followed him he explained that their continuation in the church did not confer any privilege on them. They were to serve their fellow citizens by undertaking the real work of evangelization. They were to inculcate a deeper and truly personal conviction in others, now that people had been shocked out of their complacent syncretism. And that is precisely what happened, even though Bishop Robert and his priests were expelled from Haiti. The Christian community, now a minority group, carried on the work of conscientization and fostered authentic personal conviction in others, with the result that a different and far more demanding Christianity took root in Haiti. But that is only one diocese, and there are hundreds of dioceses in Latin America that face the same problem of syncretism. It is the exception that highlights the rule.

In the first section of this chapter, I stressed the *psychological* difficulty involved in shifting from an approach that relies on captive audiences and pressure tactics to one that relies on free agents who may choose to disregard our pastoral message. Here I should like to stress another difficulty involved in shifting from protected majorities to active minorities, from the usual approach to that adopted by Bishop Robert in Haiti. And this particular difficulty is *theological* in origin. Though it is not expressed as such, the theology that pastoral agents and other people sense and live out in their daily lives can be summed up in three basic points. And each of them strongly reinforces the tendency to rely on a minimum of obligations for maintaining a maximum number of Christians.

The first assumption is that *the church has been fashioned for the benefit of those who belong to it*. In founding his church on earth, Jesus conferred on Christians the immense benefits of faith and the sacraments. Thus he created a privileged position for those who would agree to become part of his salvation community. By the same token, those in charge of the church's pastoral activity are normally responsible for their flock, the members of the church.[3] Of course some members of the church do try to serve the rest of humanity. But the rest of humanity, as such, is in the hands of divine providence rather than under the care of pastoral officials. Somehow or other every human being is offered the opportunity by God to become a part of the true church.

The second assumption of this theology is that *the*

universality of the church is quantitative, not qualitative. Some minimum qualitative factor is required, of course, for membership in the church. But aside from that, the church is destined to be universal, to enlist the adherence of each and every human being. It would be senseless, in this view, to sacrifice the church's intended universality for some qualitative requirement that could not help but be elitist and minority-oriented. If everybody is called to the church, including the poorest and the weakest, it simply is not fair or evangelical to impose demands that are beyond their strength and that are not required for membership in the church.

The third assumption of this theology is that *the church is always the best place for obtaining salvation.* In the last analysis this is the most basic reason for the pastoral approach adopted. The gospel message tells us that those who believe and are baptized will be saved. This can only mean membership in the church in the eyes of some. If other people come along and try to impose additional obligations on people, thus alienating them from the church, they must answer for the salvation or damnation of those whom they keep outside the church. At the very least they must answer for the fact that they have made people's salvation more difficult by keeping them outside the community established by Jesus himself.

Now these three assumptions may be very debatable. What cannot be denied by anyone is the fact that our traditional pastoral approach has been the logical application of those principles, and that it has opposed any improvements that would threaten those assumptions. The introduction of improvements cautiously and progressively is an approach ruled out in Latin America. But it is not ruled out by shortsightedness, conservatism, or pastoral inability; it is ruled out by the logic of the underlying theological assumptions. If we wish to get the Latin American church to shift from the protection of majorities to the development of truly Christian minorities, we must prove theologically that the three aforementioned assumptions are incorrect.

FROM CONTRACTING ALLIANCES
TO RELYING ON THE POWER OF THE GOSPEL

As we have already noted, the tacit and frequent alliances of the Latin American church with centers of political and economic power do not seem to derive from any will to political or financial power. They seem to be based on the principle of choosing the lesser evil. Since Christian majorities are in great danger of falling away from the church in modern society, it seems more prudent to protect their Christianity with the help of outside authorities.

When a military coup is effected, and such coups are usually conservative in nature, the change of political command is always supported by the prestige of the church. One of its higher-echelon representatives in the country appears alongside the new rulers, and the scene is recorded for radio, TV, and the press. Now this maneuver is not something that greatly appeals to the church official in question or promotes his own career. In most instances it is an unpleasant task for him. He knows very well that a large part of the population will find the new regime odious and against their best interests, and that they will view his participation in unfriendly terms. But if he did not add his prestige to the takeover, that would signify a break with the government and reprisals would be sure to follow. It is not that the reprisals would fall on him personally, but that they would affect the aid that the government gives to the church in one form or another to bolster its hold on the masses or its institutions.

If we were to ask that prelate why he was not willing to rely on the gospel message itself, why the church could not carry on its functions under the impetus of that message, he probably would not even understand the point of our question. Chronologically and culturally we are far removed from that ancient church that relied solely on the intrinsic force and attractiveness of the gospel message itself.[4]

It is much the same with economic power. More than one bishop in Latin America, for example, has personally chosen to take seriously the notion of "the church of the poor." More than one bishop has stopped living in the old episcopal "palace" and gone to live with the poor in their neighborhoods. But such gestures only reinforce the point I tried to make earlier. One is making a serious mistake and overlooking the real problem when one assumes that the church's alliances with economic and political powers stem from any personal desire for power or money. Nor is one justified in talking about the *personal* cowardice or conservatism of the bishops, for many of them are valiant individuals who are willing to endure poverty and imprisonment. It is what they see as the needs of the church that wins out over their own personal generosity and courage.

Take the case of the bishop who goes to live among the poor. It is almost universally true that this gesture will not mean that the episcopal palace or the curial buildings will be shut down or sold. The church, too, needs an administrative setup to handle its internal affairs. While the bishop may choose to be poor himself, the church still needs and uses considerable sums of money to maintain the organisms used to protect Christians. Schools and universities and media continue to operate, and they are visible to all. Thus the personal witness of the bishop is little more than an epiphenomenon, perhaps convincing some people that there are a few decent people even in the church. But the growing social awareness of people in Latin America is not convinced or converted by that gesture.

Another line of witness might be much more effective. Let the bishop stay in his palace. But let him also decree that the church will hand over all its institutions to the state and henceforth rely solely on the enduring power and attractiveness of Christ's good news. We do not find that line of witness in Latin America.

At this point we cannot help but raise a question: Why does such a line of witness seem so impossible to the church and its leaders? Why does that option seem so crazy that it is not even brought up for discussion? I think we must say that the shift from alliances to reliance on the gospel is not made because an underlying certainty prevents it. Underlying our present pastoral approach is the conviction that *the gospel message no longer possesses the power it once had.* And we need only point to pastoral experience itself to prove the truth of that assertion.

Whatever the reason may be, the church today knows it is impossible for it to match the performance of the early church in the area of evangelization. The Latin American church feels keenly aware of that fact. Whether one regards it as scandalous or as obvious, that conviction pervades our pastoral approach here to such an extent that the church ends up witnessing *against* the gospel message. And those who offer this counter-witness fully realize what they are doing.

This pastoral conviction, too, derives from three underlying assumptions that are taken for granted and that play an important role. The first derives from the paradoxical realization that the present difficulties facing the gospel are the result of its success. In the early days of the church people had a certain conception of Christians. It may have been overly simplistic and naive, but it was widespread. The church and its followers seemed to have a monopoly on love, and this did much to spread the gospel message to others. The gospel seemed to have a monopoly on certain authentic values.

But what impact can the gospel message have today, when everybody displays love to some extent and Christians do not seem to love more or better than anyone else? If the older image of the church and its message was true, then that message has been so successful that in the twentieth century we find numerous groups and movements espousing love, solidarity, and mutual sacrifice. Marxism itself, now the official doctrine of countries that contain more than half the world's population, proclaims the implementation of real and effective love as Christianity once did. It seeks to give equal opportunity and fulfillment to all, but disclaims all ties with religion. And it directly opposes the profit motive as a basis for social relations, associating that motive with the western capitalist world where most Christians live. In short, then, some evangelical values have become so generally known and accepted that the gospel message itself no longer has the peculiar attractiveness it once had. But dismay over the fact can only be justified if one assumes that the gospel is preached only to win adherents to the church. One can hardly be dismayed if one assumes that the proclamation of the gospel was meant to bring about such widespread recognition and acceptance of its basic values.

The second underlying assumption is simple enough,

but it would be well to spell it out. No one doubts that many people can indeed find the reason for their existence in the gospel message, even today. What is doubtful is that the number of people who reach that conviction will exceed the number of people who join other organizations, movements, and parties engaged in fellowship and united effort. And so we are back at the problem discussed earlier in this chapter. If the church relies solely on the power of the gospel message, it will only come up with a minority; and it will lose the masses. It will have a minority of strong and courageous Christians engaged in transforming society but the masses will be lost to it, and perhaps to God and salvation as well.

The third underlying assumption is most important for pastoral praxis, and we shall explore it more deeply in Chapter IV. Here we shall do no more than allude to it. When people point to concrete pastoral experience to prove that the gospel no longer possesses the attractive power it once had, the underlying assumption is that our pastoral work is presenting the very same gospel message that was proclaimed by the early church. That assumption is open to serious question. First of all, the task of proclaiming the gospel message was neglected for centuries; even while external circumstances remained largely the same, our pastoral technique got rusty. Today the world has changed greatly. Can we really be sure that we are dealing with the "good news" of Jesus every time that we talk about Jesus, his message, and the church? Only if we could prove that we are could we rely on our pastoral experience to provide evidence for our assumptions.

In any case it should be evident that there are serious obstacles and objections confronting any attempt to make the transitions discussed in this chapter. What is more, as I have said more than once, we do not yet possess any sure criteria for determining the proper choice. It is not enough to point out that the present approach is a vicious circle, for the alternative approach might be one too.

The point of interest to us here is that however serious and important the reasons militating against a shift in approach may be, they are not brought out into the open and discussed frankly. Instead they are left buried under an air of fatalism. The reasons for this will be discussed in the next chapter.

NOTES

1. See the Supplement to *La Vie Spirituelle*, no. 53, Paris, 1960, second quarter, pp. 118–19 and 126–27: "Probably the most decisive factor in this connection is the fact that most Christians today live in a society that is not unanimously Christian but rather *pluralistic*. What is more, Catholics are a minority almost everywhere, and over against Catholic moral principles stand different or opposing systems of moral values." ". . . The older casuistic approach concerned with occasions of sin and complicity, which was deeply tinged with a purely individualistic conception of salvation in the textbooks, will give way to a more constructive and positive conception of activity in the world."

2. See J.E. Monast, *On les croyait chrétiens* (Paris: Ed. du Cerf, 1969). He deals with syncretism between Christianity and the religion of the Aymaras.

3. In his well known play, *The Deputy*, Hochhuth has one character remark that "the Pope is responsible for 500 million Catholics." That is offered as the reason why the Vatican could not intervene on behalf of the Jews, and many would find it quite natural and cogent.

4. "Taking an initial look at the missionary effort of the church, we would distinguish two clearly defined periods of different length: the period prior to 315 A.D., and the period following that date. . . . In the Greco-Roman world of the apostolic era, the evangelical presence of the church was dominated by a desire to spread the gospel message to the whole world *relying solely on the impetus of the Spirit*. The Edict of Constantine inaugurated an official relationship between the church and reigning governments" (Louis and André Rétif, *Pour une Eglise en état de mission*, Je sais, je crois Series [Paris: Fayard, 1961]).

V Hidden Motives Behind the Present Pastoral Approach

Prompted by a conviction based partly on sociology and partly on the Christian faith itself, I have asserted that the vicious circle is not a fated necessity. Once we come to that position, we are forced to conclude that the only way to break the vicious circle is to opt for an entirely different approach.

From the viewpoint of history, of course, the Latin American church was the one least in a position to opt for any radical change. We have already noted that fact. Quite aside from that, however, we saw in the last chapter that a radically new option would entail certain transitions and that there might be very solid reasons militating against such shifts in approach and emphasis. I was almost tempted to say: very solid and very *respectable* reasons. But it is precisely here that we run into a problem. How solid and respectable are those reasons?

When one has solid and respectable reasons, one spells them out. Yet here, in Latin America, we are faced with a conspiracy of silence. The same thing has happened at every pastoral conference that I have attended, whether it was concerned with pastoral theology or pastoral practice. Right away everyone gets down to considering certain improvements that might be made in the existing system. But no one starts out by questioning the system as a whole and proposing an alternative approach.

Many people are consciously aware that pastoral activity in Latin America has reached an impasse, yet some instinctive antipathy prevents them from looking at what they are doing as a whole and passing judgment on it. They somehow cannot bring themselves to consider a different pastoral approach that would entail the shifts considered in the last chapter. Why?

My hypothesis here is that a threefold fearfulness weighs upon us, preventing us from considering any real alternatives. And while this fearfulness may be understandable and reasonable enough, it is not respectable. Fear is never respectable, and so we prefer to keep the fear hidden inside ourselves and whistle in the dark. That is what is happening to pastoral activity in Latin America.

WE ARE FEARFUL FOR OURSELVES

In the previous chapter I discussed the shift from exerting pressure to nurturing personal liberty. My aim was to shed light on the factual situation, not to formulate values; but I could feel myself proposing a value judgment. Who, after all, would dare to *say* that they preferred pressure to personal liberty?

Yet concrete experience shows that we do in fact prefer the pressure to liberty in practice, though we may not be willing to admit it. The examples cited in the last chapter clearly bring out that preference, and they point up the terrible insecurity of pastoral agents who have not been trained to deal with people who are free rather than pressured. Consider for a moment everything that pastoral agents know and routinely speak about in their work. Now what happens when they happen to run into a stranger and begin to converse? Do they not usually end up talking about some incidental topic such as sports or the weather? But if that is to be our concrete experience with the freedom of another, if that is to be the normal occupation of a whole lifetime, who could put up with it? No one, I expect, and we all seem to know that from the start.

But consider the present situation of the priest specifically. Up until a few years ago there was a certain social consensus about his ordination and its purpose, and it even found expression in the ordination rites. The hands of the priest were sacred, and so were his functions. By that very fact they were also necessary, and hence the priest did not have to compete with other professionals or technicians on the same plane. His competence was of a different order.

Contrast this with the situation of the ordinary professional. His competence is based on some sort of proficiency that can be measured and can be maintained only by continual practice and study. If doctors start killing their patients, they will not remain doctors for long. If they do not stay abreast of new developments in medicine, they will lose the respect and trust of their patients. They cannot rely solely on what they learned twenty-five years ago.

Once upon a time the priesthood seemed to rescue its recipients from all those contingencies. The sacred efficacy that flowed from the hands of the priest did not depend on personal ability, competence, or further study. It was there, embedded in his hands once and for all. His was a profession with guaranteed success and no danger of failure; and so the priest stood outside the anxiety-ridden struggle to make a living that shapes the psychology of contemporary people.

Now the priest was suddenly forced to confront this

same anxiety, magnified a hundredfold, even though his training had not undergone any change. There is always an element of anxiety in espousing oneself to the freedom of other people, but at least other professionals possess tried techniques and skills that are deemed valuable and necessary. All the priest has to offer people is an innocent call to complicate their lives further. Aside from the fact that he had not been trained to deal with people as free agents, his whole previous life had been spent in routine activities that turned him into a more or less bureaucratic agent. Now he was supposed to give all that up for something new and unfamiliar to him.

No examples are really necessary to help one appreciate the impact of this new situation. But I offer one here to highlight its psychological impact on priests and its potential scope in Latin American pastoral activity. Studies in one Catholic university revealed that students did not like to attend obligatory classes in religion and that loss of faith was frequent among them. One professor suggested an alternative approach to the religious curriculum. Let the university create an institute of religious studies that would explore the principal problems of the faith in connection with the various professional studies offered at the university. Classes at the new institute would be electives, and students could select those classes that seemed most related to their own field of study. As the professor explained his proposal to the rest of the faculty, he noticed that three elderly priests were weeping. On the way out he asked a colleague if he knew what the problem was. His colleague explained that they were weeping out of anger and frustration. The three priests had been appointed to their teaching posts because they held theology degrees and because religion classes were *obligatory* at the university. If religion classes were made optional, they were absolutely certain that not a single student would come to their classes. They would no longer have any usefulness, and their lives would be without purpose or meaning. But how could they put that into words?

This example brings up another factor producing anxiety. Aside from fear of failure, there is the feeling of insecurity connected with *one's material means of support*. Insofar as priestly functions are concerned, we do well to note the curious problem involved. Basically there are two general types of priestly functions. In one set of functions the priest essentially *repeats* the same ritual formulas that he learned before his ordination and that are inscribed in the liturgical books. In the other set of functions he basically expresses his own creative effort in absorbing and communicating the Christian message. He gives sermons, holds conferences, directs church groups, and offers counselling. Up to now the age-old prudence of the church has determined that the priest's material support should be bound up with his *repetitive* functions rather than his creative ones. A shift of emphasis to the latter functions, then, would entail a direct attack on his wonted means of sustenance. It is not just that dialogue with a free agent is likely to end up in failure nine times out of ten. It is that the priest's *material* support is headed for ruin if it is to be based on the success or failure of such creative efforts. And precisely because it has to do with his material life, the priest finds it all the harder to express his anxiety about it.

To put it briefly once again, any major shift from the use of pressure to reliance on people's free will and decision would entail great material and psychological anxiety for most members of the clergy, and similar anxiety for other people engaged in pastoral work. It is this fact that explains why certain things are left *unsaid* when pastoral activity comes up for discussion. The fact

WE ARE FEARFUL FOR THE SALVATION OF THE MASSES

By "masses" here I do not mean any particular social class. If we make the shift from protecting artificial majorities to cultivating heroic minorities, then the *majority* of people will be left without protection and without a minimal level of Christianity. The term "masses" refers to that majority here, the emphasis being on their basic passivity. The fact is that their present participation in Christianity is basically a passive one, produced by artificial Christian environments that are maintained by the church's pastoral agents. And I make this point at the start because here there is an unspoken reason that makes it all the more difficult for people to come out and ask why the church must continue with a pastoral approach based on the protection of passive majorities.

The curious fact is that in the documents of the Medellín Conference we find two different conceptions of what is meant by the term "masses." When it deals with pastoral concern for elites, the term "masses" means one thing; when it deals specifically with pastoral care of the masses, the term means something very different. In the document dealing with pastoral care of elites, the elites are defined in terms of their social *status*. The "masses," therefore, are all those who do not have special training, technical skills, and responsibilities in society. Thus here the term "masses" is surrounded with all the positive connotations usually associated with the term "the people," or even with the term "the poor and lowly" (since rich people usually have special training and societal responsibilities).

In the document dealing specifically with the masses, however, the term "masses" does not refer to the poor as such but to the passive majorities we have just mentioned. Thus the masses are not defined in terms of their social status in this document. The "masses" here would include both poor and rich, professionals and non-professionals. The stress in this document is on *motivation* as the factor defining who belongs to the masses. Their motives for embracing the faith are mixed, and there is a large dose of egotism involved.

Inadvertent readers might move from one document to the other with the assumption that they are complementary. Perhaps a bit disturbed with the document on pastoral concern for elites, they might want to know what the church intends to do for the masses—for the people as a whole or the poor. Yet the second document, using the same terms, actually proposes a pastoral effort that remains sympathetic to the same rich people covered in the first document. For it is the rich, after all, whose involvement in Christianity is most bound up with self-interest.

A concrete example may help to bring out my point here. About seven or eight years ago the directors of a Catholic university in Brazil discovered that five young Communists had infiltrated the student body. A meeting was promptly called, and the directors agreed that the five students should be expelled because they represented a danger for the rest of the student body.

It is not the particulars of this case that are of interest to us here. It is rather the universal features that typify the Latin American situation. One may disagree with the decision of the university board to expel the five students, but at the same time one must recognize how well founded their fear was in sociological terms. The fact is that five Communist students did constitute a danger for the protected majority of students, whether they were one thousand or five thousand. Why? Not because the five were Communists, but because they were a heroic minority in the midst of the student masses. *Mutatis mutandis*, five convinced Christians could represent a similar threat at Moscow University.

A second point is worth noting here. The decision of the faculty board did not go so far as to question the overall pastoral approach at the university. But of what value could that effort at the university be, if several thousand Catholic students could not possibly represent a threat to the five Communists and their beliefs? The conclusion is clear enough. The underlying theology behind this pastoral effort assumes that the Christians' reason for being is found within themselves; it has nothing to do with some function of service to the rest of humankind.

And that brings us to a third point. However clear-cut and consistent the underlying theology may be, it never surfaces in open and frank discussion. Why? Undoubtedly one important change in church outlook has something to do with it. Though certain texts of Vatican II remain somewhat ambiguous, its basic thrust runs counter to any such theology and therefore inhibits open formulation or discussion of it. That at least is how many people see it, and so one cannot so readily espouse dogmas that actually underlie the classic pastoral approach.

But there is a further difficulty here, and it has to do with the terminology we have been considering. In what category are we to place the five thousand students of the Catholic university in question? Are they to be included under "elites" or "masses"? Paradoxically enough, they belong to both categories and our pastoral effort converges on them from both directions. They are part of the "elite" insofar as fortune, professional training, and responsible social position are concerned; they are part of the "masses" insofar as their Christian motives are very mixed and their adhesion to the church is based mainly on the factor of protection. Discussion of our basic pastoral approach and its underlying theology is sidestepped; it is replaced with vague or ill-defined terms that have judgmental overtones.

Another case might be cited here. Cardinal Jean Daniélou wrote a book that was well received by pastoral officials in Latin America. It considered prayer as a political problem, and it furnished our pastoral officials with terms and idioms to justify their existing approach.[1] The point I want to consider here is the fact that in stressing that some people must be protected by the church or else they will cease to be Christians, Daniélou injects a term that has profound human and biblical resonance. He talks about "the poor."

Now this term itself is almost designed to exercise *verbal terrorism* over possible dissenters. No one would really dare to speak out against "the poor." But Daniélou knew very well that "the poor" of whom he was speaking in his book had little or nothing to do with "the poor" as understood by society or the Bible. It is obvious enough that his "poor" people who needed church protection were not equivalent to those who are economically poor. That they were not "the poor" of the Bible may not be so readily clear.

Daniélou argued that if we did not have church institutions to protect Christians, large numbers of them would stop being Christians. Only the strong, the elite, would make up the church. Here it is apparent that Daniélou is using the word "poor" as a synonym for the word "weak." His concern is for those who would be too weak to maintain their faith without institutional support.

But what about "the poor of Yahweh" in the Bible? Are they weak in their convictions? Certainly not, and Daniélou knows that as well as anyone. The "poor of Yahweh" were those who fixed their hopes on Yahweh alone and remained loyal to him despite countless temptations to betrayal and despair. In the prophetical writings of the Bible, therefore, the "poor of Yahweh" are not the vast majority of the Israelites but God's "remnant."[2] They make up a heroic minority of strong-willed people.

Here I am not trying to decide for the church what pastoral approach it should adopt. My point is simply to show where our fearfulness for the salvation of artificial Christian majorities leads us. It makes us suspicious of any other possible approach. And if we try to present a pastoral or theological justification for a radically different approach, our very words are criticized for being *elitist*. Once again fear keeps us from bringing the motives behind our pastoral approach out into the open.

WE ARE FEARFUL FOR THE GOSPEL

Here again we face a psychological block that affects our pastoral effort. After all, who would dare to face the fact of the church's alliances and admit that it is unwilling to rely solely on the power of the gospel message? Hardly anyone would deny that in Latin America the church feels compelled to accept or endorse certain things that it would not really choose to accept or endorse if it could have things its own way.[3] If it lived in a desert, or if it could prevent them without any repercussions on itself, it certainly would not ally itself with the forces responsible for them.

Now suppose some puzzled or surprised party should ask why the church feels obliged to accept things that it ought to reject. Confronted with such a question, the church's only response is silence. Or else people say that the church must exercise prudence, which comes down to almost the same thing. "Prudence," after all, is not exercised in a vacuum. It considers all the risks involved in a certain course of action and then comes to a decision. Exactly what "risk" is it, then, that urges "prudence" on the church in Latin America?

There is little discussion of that question, but the answer is clear enough: If the church refused to endorse certain actions of the state, the whole weight of government authority might be brought to bear against it; or else it might have to close down all its institutions serving mass Christianity for lack of financial resources. The risk, in other words, is that the church might be reduced to reliance on the gospel message alone. There is little discussion of the issue precisely because no one wants to admit that this is the risk that the church is trying to avoid by relying on prudence instead. Once again a key element in our pastoral activity is left out of our discussions.

But the facts are a bit more complicated. The above remarks apply well enough to the more obvious forms of alliance and connivance designed to safeguard typical Christian institutions. Besides those institutions, however, today we find a whole gamut of "pastoral" activities that are of a more distinct and special nature. A concrete example will help us to grasp the picture.

At one point there was a meeting of foreign-born priests who had worked in Latin America for some length of time. Much to their surprise, they suddenly realized that most of their work in Latin America was not dictated by pastoral criteria but simply by what we would call *human compassion*.

That in itself might well be expected. Everyone knows that Latin America contains a goodly portion of the world's undernourished population. About half of its population is illiterate, and there is widespread ignorance about such fields as hygiene, law, documentary procedures, and civil rights. In many rural areas, particularly those inhabited by aborigines, a feudal and almost slavish structure predominates. Such is the human panorama that foreign-born missionaries confront, and it cannot help but have a powerful impact on them. They discover a vast multitude of fellow human beings who need almost everything and who are ready to ask for anything—for anything except the gospel message.

Thanks to training and general standard of living, almost any priest or religious can help. If they come from more affluent countries, they can also mobilize the resources of their native countries to assist Latin Americans. Basically, then, those priests and religious do not start out by trying to prepare people to hear the gospel message. Their initial step is a warm, human, and Christian reaction to the problems and questions of fellow humans who are suffering. But it is only a short step from there to making use of this aid for pastoral purposes. Pastoral *utilization* of the proffered aid is a ready temptation. What is more, one's pastoral work necessarily takes on a certain orientation when it is linked up with other forms of aid, particularly when the recipients cannot do without that aid.

Now some might say that in such circumstances human beings cannot be free anyway, so why worry about the link? To that we can only reply by asking two further questions: (1) Do people become free human beings through this particular approach? (2) In such an approach is the gospel truly a message of good news for the recipients, or is it simply a new kind of alignment?

Be that as it may, it should be obvious that we find it enormously difficult to give solid expression to our central pastoral attitudes. One serious and central question, for example, is whether Christ meant the gospel message to be addressed to people living in the subhuman circumstances that affect many Latin Americans. God waited until humankind had been around for at least a couple of million years before he sent Christ. This suggests that his decision was not prompted merely by compassion; God chose a moment when the gospel would be useful and appropriate in history. Yet who dares to raise this basic question, though Christianity has been around for twenty centuries and many countries claim to be Christian?[4]

We are confronted with a confused mass of facts, and an even more confused welter of language. People seem to talk almost indiscriminately about the good news, human misery, Christian aid, and pastoral works designed to serve people's most urgent needs. Once again we sense a fear that the gospel message on its own has little to say and even less to attract people in Latin America. It is lost on the rich because they are rich, and the poor because they are poor.

So far we have been talking in terms of individuals for the most part. Today, however, the whole issue has taken on continental dimensions. In the decade of the sixties the Latin American church began to receive impressive sums of money for developmental programs from churches in the developed countries. That in turn led some Latin American governments to entrust similar tasks to the Latin American church, or at least to make sure that it could carry out that work without fear of competition or hindrance. Again we are faced with the basic problem we have been considering, only now it is even more generalized. Faced with the poverty, ignorance, and substandard living conditions of many Latin Americans, the hierarchical church assumed the task of promoting human development.

This generalized situation forces us to look at the attendant problems and ask some questions. And we must begin with problems of terminology. What are we to say about the institutions for human betterment run by the church? Are they *Christian institutions* in the sense we have defined above? Do they, in other words, combine a civic goal (human betterment) with a pastoral or ecclesial goal?

Some people, recalling that the church possessed similar functions in an older era when all societal institutions conspired to support Christian faith and practice, have spoken of the newer institutions as instances of a "New Christendom." In organizing new institutions for human and societal development, the church is recreating the social order that once predominated in the West and was called Christendom.

It is obvious, however, that the newer institutions are markedly different in some respects from such classic Christian institutions as parochial schools, hospitals, and the religious press. First of all, the newer institutions seem to be prompted by human and Christian compassion rather than by any specifically pastoral principle. The example of the Good Samaritan is in the background as church officials contemplate the plight of their fellow citizens. They do not want to imitate the priest and the scribe in that story.

In this case it is suggested that the church is not allying itself with the government but simply standing in as a replacement for some other organism or body that could in theory do this work of social service but does not in fact exist. It is not an *alliance,* therefore, implying that the church is afraid to trust in the power of the gospel message alone. Rather, the church is acting as a *replacement* or *substitute* for other people or institutions that are not present. That is why the hierarchy chooses to take on this work of human promotion even though it does not fall within the range of its proper functions. The members of the church's hierarchy are not acting here as such, but rather as human beings and Christians who are deeply moved by the plight of their fellow Latin Americans.

Here again verbal terrorism can come into play when someone objects to the idea that the hierarchy of the church should have charge of this task to the exclusion of other groups. After all, the church is supposed to be "the church of the poor," a church engaged in serving others and sharing the joys and sorrows of humankind. How could one dare to oppose that notion or its concrete implementation? The sanction against such a negative view of the church's role in this area is all the more powerful in that those in charge of such projects can acquire broad power of an international nature both inside and outside the church. As some recent episcopal appointments indicate, that power may be very real and have little to do with one's pastoral merits.

Even if we accept the basic notion that the church is acting as a replacement here rather than forming any alliances, we are still faced with the fact that it must neglect its own proper task to the extent that it fills in for someone else. We have already noted the lack of personnel in Latin America and the inability of the church to get out of the vicious circle. Its work of replacement only aggravates that basic situation, unless those who use that term actually do not see it in terms of "replacement" or "substitution" at all.

But let us get away from vague suspicions and try to focus on certain facts that may provide us with a more objective picture. Faced with the fact that the church has assumed the task of promoting human betterment in Latin America, we can raise a number of questions. Here I shall raise five basic ones. It has been my personal experience that the usual answers to these questions are either incorrect or inadequate, suggesting that we are dealing here with an alliance rather than with some form of substitution.

The first basic question is this: *Is the church the only possible group or force capable of offering this aid?* If it is not, then it is obvious that we are dealing with the classic mechanism of the Christian institution rather than with some form of substitution.

There is some solid foundation for the question asked. However underdeveloped the nations of Latin America may be, they are not back in the Middle Ages. In the big cities we find many groups with different ideologies and programs; and these groups are ready and willing to move into action. If the church wishes to maintain that it is merely standing in for nonexisting organisms, it must be able to show that it is the only group capable of providing the aid in question.

One common but inadequate response to this question is that the church is the only organism capable of furnishing this aid because the state allows the church to operate in this area but does not allow other groups to do so. Obviously in such a case we are not dealing with substitution at all. We are confronted with a matter of *competition*, in which other ideological groups are taken out of the market by the state. Moreover, there are clear-cut political connotations in the fact that the state gives the church exclusive rights over this task—all the more clear-cut when Marxist or revolutionary groups are among the competitors. The work of human promotion done by the church is permitted because the assumption is that it will not create problems for the socio-political status quo. Not only is it not a real substitute for the work of others; it is also seen as complicity with the ideology and existing order of the state. As consciousness-raising increases, people will not fail to point out that fact; and that is what the real significance of the church will be in the eyes of many people.

Yet some will still maintain that such human promotion is a task that cannot be put off. The response to that assertion, which can and is being made, is that such reformism is actually a powerful enemy of the real revolution that is called for. To the extent that certain needs and urgencies are satisfied within the framework of the established order, the urgency of changing that order is diminished.

Here I am not trying to work up any definitive value judgment about the situation under analysis. It may be necessary to carry on with such activities. But the pastoral scene would be greatly cleared up if we realized that we are dealing here with an alliance, not with some form of replacement or substitution.

The second basic question is this: *Does the aid and other work of human promotion undertaken by the church effectively reach everybody independently of their ideologies and religious creeds?* If these aid programs tended to favor Christians mainly or exclusively, then obviously the church is not acting as a substitute here solely because the urgency of people's needs has motivated it to fulfill that role.

The usual response to this question is a round "yes." The church, it is asserted, does not require that people be Christians in order to obtain this aid. But here again we are dealing with a half-truth. There are countless ways of engaging in discrimination without it being explicitly or formally espoused.

For example, aid programs involving food distribution are common throughout the Latin American continent. When such programs go through the parish priest, the food distribution almost cannot help but take place at meetings and local centers of Christians. When the parish priest gets people to handle the distribution, he usually calls upon people who are close to himself. Information and reports on people's needs operate through channels of friendly interchange and conversation, so that exclusivism tends to take over in practice. In one instance a baby died of malnutrition even though its home was only a few short steps away from a church where food was being distributed. Clearly the channels of communication and information are not open equally to all. But in this instance there was a further fact to note. When the child's parents were asked why they had not had recourse to the food donations offered by the local church, they replied that they did not share the same ideas.

Now one may differ with that point of view, but there is no doubt that the importance attached to ideological differences does constitute an intrinsic kind of human development and growth. Thus the more truly human people become in Latin America, the more discrimination will be found with regard to the aid offered by the church. By the same token, if such discrimination really does not come into play, it can only be because we are maintaining a pre-ideological stage that is itself out of line with real human betterment.

We seem to run up against a two-edged open-mindedness here. On the one hand people seem to be open to the idea that this aid should reach everyone; on the other they seem to calmly accept the fact that it does not really reach all. Thus there does not seem to be any strong safeguard against the pressure that such aid might exercise, at least so long as the pressure involved has something to do with membership in the church. Lacking solid proof to the contrary, therefore, we must challenge the notion that the church is merely acting as a replacement here. At the very least we must bring the issue out in the open instead of passing over it in silence.

A third basic question might well be asked: *When churches in foreign countries do send aid supplies and provisions, couldn't these be handed over directly to representatives of the recipient communities?* Why do they have to go through the hands of hierarchical figures in the church?

What is happening now is somewhat akin to what goes on with food tins and other items supplied to poor countries by the United States. Plastered all over the crates and tins in many different languages is the notice: "Donated by the people of the United States." This, you see, prevents any fraudulent use of the donations for propaganda purposes by others. So when churches in foreign countries send similar aid and have it administered through the Catholic hierarchy, it is as if they were trying to make sure that people would know that the supplies were "donated by the Catholic church."

When it is suggested that the aid might be placed directly in the hands of civil officials and local leaders, the classic response is that they are not really responsible and honest people; that they would be tempted to favor certain groups or to promote their own selfish interests.

Here again the response is not satisfactory. First of all, answering on the most superficial level, we can say that all the different organisms involved in international aid possess checks and controls to ensure against possible abuses. To get down closer to the heart of the matter, we must realize that if political officials are not responsible individuals, then the only worthwhile change must take place on the political level. If it does not take place there, then the existing situation will not only be hopeless and without solution; as even the most conservative sociologists acknowledge, an apolitical approach actually means support of the status quo.

If we attempt to solve certain problems without tackling the existing flaws on the political level, our aid work will not only make a mockery of development but also obstruct it even more. A concrete example of this whole problem, and of the offbase answers given to this third question and the following one, is to be found in the experience of one parish in Chile. Foreign aid arrived in the neighborhood, and it was to be distributed by the church. After spending some time in personally handling the distribution of these foodstuffs, the parish priest decided it was not really his job and that he was pressuring people to some extent at least. He called together some of his active lay parishioners and handed over the work to them. Soon these lay people came to realize that pressure was being exerted if only one group distributed the goods. They told the parish priest they wanted to call a meeting of all the community leaders, of whatever ideological persuasion, so that they might be able to decide how to distribute the aid equitably in the area. The parish priest agreed. Some time later the Catholic lay leaders came back to tell the priest what had happened. For the first time all the natural leaders in the area had come together. They began to give serious thought to the serious problems in the community, and the key problem seemed to be the foreign aid itself. Without this foreign aid and the difficulties it raised, real *political* activity and responsibility might be developed among the people. And that was the course they all preferred.

The example may be one in a million, but its value is not on the statistical level. It strongly suggests that there is no real remedy for the problems confronting Latin America unless the people of Latin America develop political awareness and a real sense of political responsibility, as peoples in more developed countries did in the past. Any attempt to set aside the issue of political action is itself political in its overtones; it is politically conservative.

This point dovetails with the one brought out in connection with the first question. There we noted that some people claim the church is the only organism able to administer foreign aid because the existing government will not let any other organism handle it. But why is that so? Because existing regimes do not see the church as a threat to the status quo.

In objective terms, then, we are confronted with an <u>alliance</u> here. What is more, we must realize that certain kinds of "substitute" work may be worse than the problem itself. It is quite possible that some types of aid may actually be opiates. The supposed cure may be worse than the disease, for it only covers up the disease without eliminating the root cause.

The fourth basic question might be put thus: *Couldn't lay people take charge of these human development tasks that are now in the hands of bishops and priests?* If the tasks in question do represent some sort of substitute work on the part of the church, a negative answer to this question would have to be based on the same notion or justification mentioned above: No, lay people cannot be entrusted with these tasks because they are not sufficiently honest or responsible.[5]

Experience, however, does not justify any such assumption. Religious figures have been no less adept than the laity in closing their eyes to certain irregularities, in finding legal loopholes, and in tapping bureaucratic sources of influence. What is more, they tend to exert greater influence and to be tolerated more by government authorities.

Insofar as native competence is concerned, we can find a pertinent example in the running of a classic Christian institution like the Catholic university. In Latin America the rectors of such universities are, with very rare exceptions, members of the hierarchy. Only a few of these clergymen have university training equivalent to that of most professors on the faculties of these universities. They have spent much of their lives in other areas of work, and so they are not familiar with the problems faced by the university. So why are they in charge of the Catholic universities? It can hardly be to defend and preserve orthodoxy because religion classes are given by priests; and if there is a theology department, it has its own dean and clerical authorities.

There are two convergent reasons for this phenomenon, as we learn from a meeting of experts summoned by CELAM (the Latin American Episcopal Conference) to discuss the matter of "the Christian presence in the university." First of all, laypeople must give due consideration to their peers, and hence to an extent democratize the management of a university on certain levels. Only a clergyman can maintain a strictly vertical management, hiring and firing professors at will.

The full import of that reason, however, comes out clearly only in connection with the more general and pervasive reason. What basically the present setup seeks to prevent is the *politicization* of the Catholic university. An apolitical stance is practically its whole reason for being, both in the eyes of many parents and in the eyes of many government officials. Indeed the latter may often promote Catholic universities and oppose their own civil universities, which are critical and quite politicized. A clergyman is a better bet than a layperson if one wants a rector who will resist the pressure to politicize that will be exerted by intellectuals and students in exploited regions such as Latin America. And if this apolitical thrust is to be real and effective, one must have the vertical authority structure mentioned above.

As we noted earlier, this so-called apolitical stance is actually a conservative politics disguised as neutrality. And so the appointment of hierarchical officials to management posts in the university structure constitutes a political act and a political alliance.[6]

Now that is exactly what is happening with the projects for human development that we have been discussing here. Take the case of the Basic Education Movement (MEB) in Brazil, for example. While it was in the hands of laypeople, the conscientization (that is to say, consciousness-raising) which it aimed at had strong overtones of political criticism. Government authorities reacted, not by closing down the movement itself but by putting it directly in the hands of Catholic bishops.

Here again I am not trying to make any final decision about the validity or timeliness of the institutions in question. I am simply insisting that we must discuss these issues frankly and honestly. While such institutions may begin as a form of substitution, it seems to me that they end up being much more in the nature of an alliance.

The fifth and final basic question is this: *Would the church continue to lend its support to these institutions if they were taken over by non-Christian leaders?* The question is logical enough since it is claimed that the church's involvement is a replacement for that of others. But the answer I receive to this question is that the church would not continue to lend its support so that those institutions could not be used for alien ideologies.

This response is a clear admission that people are aware of the pressure exerted by these human development programs. If someone were to claim that such pressure is not used when the church is in charge, we could still point out that there is at least a negative pressure involved in the fact that other parties are prevented from using such pressure against the church.

Obviously in such a case one can hardly talk about replacement or substitution, about simple human and

Christian concern for the needs of fellow human beings, when no one else does such work. But my questions and criticisms do not mean that I am ready to spell out what we ought to do. I simply want to insist that we must bring our fears out into the open. Those fears may be reasonable enough, but they should not be kept hidden.

To sum up, we are beset with unconfessed fears. Psychologically we are fearful for ourselves in the face of other people's freedom. Theologically we are fearful for the salvation of the masses if they are deprived of protective institutions. Pastorally we are fearful for the gospel message, suspecting that it does not have the power it once had to attract people on its own. These are the hidden but decisive motives underlying most of our pastoral activities in Latin America.

NOTES

1. The original title in French was *L'oraison, problème politique*. For various reactions to it see *Informaciones Católicas Internacionales*, no. 244, July 22, 1965. In particular see the article by Peuchmaurd entitled "La Iglesia no es un pueblo al lado de los otros."

2. "For then will I remove from your midst the proud braggarts, and you shall no longer exalt yourself on my holy mountain. But I will leave as a remnant in your midst a people humble and lowly, who shall take refuge in the name of the Lord" (Zeph. 3:11–12).

3. As Paul Tillich points out forcefully in *The Protestant Era* (Chapter 12), religion has often been nothing more than the superfluous consecration of some situation or action that was in no way judged or transformed by the consecration. Religion consecrated the feudal order and its own participation in it, without transcending it. Religion consecrated nationalism without transforming it. Religion consecrated war and its weapons wthout using its spiritual arms against war. Religion consecrated peace and its attendant security without posing any spiritual threat to it. Religion consecrated the bourgeois ideal of the family without passing judgment on it, and it consecrated various systems of exploitation without transcending them. Indeed it used these systems to its own advantage.

4. See J.L. Segundo, *De la sociedad a la teologia* (Buenos Aires: Lohlé, 1970), part IV.

5. Not to mention more ignoble motives. When one bishop was asked the reason for these institutions, he replied: "If there were no such institutions in which to place my priests, my seminary would empty out." While the remark may be apocryphal, the problem is a very real sociological one.

6. See the remarks by John Hilton in his article "Las Universidades Yanquis," in *América Latina*, Buenos Aires, August 14, 1968: "A curious interchange has been taking place since World War II. Dissatisfied with the dehumanized state of North American academic culture and education, liberal professors and students have pointed out certain disagreeable features of our own university system. In trying to correct them they have moved toward the same solution adopted by Hispanoamerican institutions under the impact of the earlier liberalizing movement. In the meantime conservatives, the armed forces, the Catholic church, and North American commercial interests have become disturbed by the ineffectiveness of the liberal university system. These parties have been pressuring and almost forcing Latin American universities to adopt the traditional structure of the North American university. To hasten success, they have sought to establish new universities which, for want of a better term, can be said to be 'North Americanized.' The power elite in Latin America and North American commercial interests support these institutions, which are run by the Catholic church—considered a bulwark against Communism. . . . The thrust of North American influence in Latin America has been to strengthen the hand of the Catholic church in university affairs."

VI   A Different Approach

I have repeatedly insisted that I possess no criteria for passing any final judgment on the facts described and opting for one of the two alternatives mentioned. Yet I fear that more than one reader assumes that I have made a choice insofar as I have indicated that one possible option is a blind alley or a vicious circle. Some readers, particularly those committed to this option, may well feel that my very presentation of the facts and my use of language clearly indicates my own choice; or that at the very least I am espousing the *negative* option of getting rid of the traditional pastoral approach.

It is probably useless to try to argue against such feelings and impressions. But let me say once again that my basic stance here is that we must not bury the issues in silence. We must call things by their right name and stop pretending that we are doing things for one set of reasons when the actual reasons are quite different. It is not at all surprising that we should be fearful in the face of the awesome changes that are going on in Latin America. That is quite logical and reasonable. It is also not surprising that we should be frightened by the radical nature of the pastoral changes required to keep pace with those awesome changes. The only illogical and unreasonable thing is to pretend that there is no possible radical alternative to the present approach.

While my exposition may have pointed toward a different pastoral approach and suggested names for it, so far it has been a negative exposition for the most part. It is easy enough to see where the existing pastoral approach and its mechanisms lead us, for we can point to hard facts. It is not so easy to see the basic mechanisms of the other possible alternative.

Let me frankly admit all that, even though the headings and subheadings of the previous chapters suggest the outlines of an alternative pastoral approach. It is for that very reason that I would like to use this chapter to outline the overall dimensions of a more positive approach. To be specific, I would like to spell out the basic focus for the alternative approach mentioned in the previous chapters. What would be the basic work of our pastoral effort within that new framework? What does it presuppose in the concrete? To what extent is it already being fleshed out in Latin America?

EVANGELIZATION AS THE PRIMARY TASK

Forced to select a term, I find that the term "evangelization" best suits our purpose here. Another Greek term, *kerygma* ("proclamation") might also be used, but several reasons make it less suitable for our purposes. The four Gospels constitute a literary genre that is usually called "kerygmatic." Moreover, the object of kerygmatic proclamation is the "good news," which is a precise translation of the term "gospel" (*euangelion* in Greek). Thus I prefer the term evangelization here because it gets right to the point and helps to define the content of our proclamation. And that is what I shall try to do in greater detail here.

A fine descriptive definition of what I understand by evangelization here can be found in Seumois's description of the three elements that go to make up authentic kerygma. This adviser to the Sacred Congregation for the Propagation of the Faith says that authentic evangelization or kerygma consists in: (1) communicating only the essentials of the Christian message; (2) communicating it as good news; and (3) adding nothing further except at a pace that will allow the essential element to remain precisely that.

Here I shall examine each of these features and try to relate them to the pastoral facts narrated in the earlier chapters.

1. Communicating only the essentials of the Christian message. This becomes imperative if we choose to shift from exerting pressure on people to relying on the liberty of adults and respecting that liberty. The fact is that if we do give up all use of pressure, we also give up something that has made our pastoral work much easier. For we have been used to detaining our listeners as long as we wanted, whether they were really interested or not. The new approach poses a real challenge to our pastoral activity, for it would have to rely on the interest it could arouse during one of the fleeting encounters that are part of societal life.

This means that we could no longer begin to transmit the Christian message with just any one of the elements, however authentic, that Christian experience and thought have been accumulating over the course of twenty centuries. In effect the new challenge brings us back to the situation of the early church. We must be able to transmit the *essential* message of Christianity within a very restricted span of time—one that our interlocutor can tolerate without looking for an excuse to bid us adieu.

This does not mean that the task in question is directly

and primarily incumbent on the priest. Insofar as he primarily has *internal* functions within the church, his job is to form a community capable of carrying out the task. Thus both the priest and the community must rediscover the essential ingredients of the gospel message. To some extent these ingredients have been buried under a welter of other elements. While these may also be true and authentic, they were piled on indiscriminately over the centuries by a church that had *plenty of time* to initiate each generation of Christians no matter which element it started with.

Today that situation is of the past. If the church cannot formulate the essential message of Christianity in the course of a typical conversation running no more than a half-hour, then there simply will be no evangelization. It cannot count on weeks, months, or years. Needless to say, many pastoral officials rely on the belief that at least the family and the Catholic school do have the time to transmit the gospel message without confining themselves to its essentials only. They forget two things. One is that even if the Christian message is transmitted to children, that no longer means that adults will really "know the gospel." This point will be considered in more detail shortly. The other is that the time available to the family and the school is also a time when the mass communications media can interefere and disrupt any such transmission of the message.

Now let us suppose that we were to ask pastoral officials this question: What is the essential message of the Christian faith? What would be their response to this natural question which is of such critical importance today? My feeling is that the question would take most of them by surprise. Perhaps it would even be most disturbing to those with the greatest and longest pastoral experience. We might get answers such as these: "that God raised his son, Jesus Christ, from the dead"; "that Jesus is the Son of God"; or "the truths formulated in the Creed."

What are we to think of these responses? That brings us to the second element described by Seumois.

2. *Communicating it as good news.* This element makes it clear that the above formulas, however brief and correct they may be, however much they may represent the essence of the Christian message, do not constitute the content of an authentic evangelization. Unlike the situation at the first level described above, at this second level it does us no good to examine the earliest professions of Christian faith.[1] Why is this? Because either they were fashioned for profession *within* the bosom of the church (against heresies, for cultic worship, and so forth), or else they were responses to questions and expectations of *their own day.*

But the *gospel* of Jesus Christ is either good news *right here and now* or else it simply is not the gospel of Jesus Christ—however orthodox may be the formula of the Creed employed. There is no evangelization when Christianity is understood to be a restrictive condition imposed by God for the attainment of salvation, a restrictive condition to which we must bow even though life is complicated by faith and the practices it entails.

If we are talking to a person whose problems and expectations are unknown to us, it is not enough to say: Do you know that God resurrected his son, Jesus Christ? With that remark we have not yet even begun the task of evangelization. The remark may be true, but our interlocutor might well say that he knows lots of other news that is much better.

One thing should be clear by now from all that we have said. Our fearfulness that the gospel message does not have the drawing power it had once upon a time is based on a real experience that is doubly false. It is false because we do not actually give people the essential message of Christianity and because we do not give that message as good news. It is not surprising, then, that it seems to be pastoral suicide to take the risk of fostering and relying on the freedom of our interlocutor in the proclamation of the gospel message.

From a more positive perspective we can say that two practical consequences flow from our second point. The first is that a message can be good news only if it relates to some expectation. Any evangelization process, therefore, must begin with *listening*, which runs counter to all our habitual reflexes and habits. Our customary assumption has been that evangelizing means talking and, insofar as it is possible, keeping our listeners quiet so that they may pay attention to our complete and logical exposition.

By "listening" here, I am not referring solely to an act on the level of the individual alone. Insofar as the Christian community is concerned, "listening" must be translated into a friendly and thoroughgoing sharing of life with the non-Christian. It must entail a shared historical sensitivity, shared commitments, and the recognition of the human values that the non-Christian holds and cultivates. This recognition, in turn, must be fleshed out in deeds.

Obviously such a context is directly opposed to any context in which Christians are set apart for the sake of their own protection. Yet only such a context can provide the foundation for an authentic process of evangelization, one in which people's deepest expectations are met by a Christian message which is truly good news for them.

And that brings us to the second practical consequence of this point. If our efforts to renew our contact with the essential message of Christianity is to be fruitful, it cannot end up in *prefabricated formulas*. A Christian community truly engaged in evangelization is one that *translates* any such rediscovered formulas into something that is capable of meeting the concrete expectations of contemporary listeners. No Christian community can operate mechanically here, much less be content to bring in the priest when someone begins to express an interest in the content of the Christian message. The Christian community must be creative.

In the religious world of Old Testament and pagan times, the good news could be formulated and expressed thus: "God raised his son, Jesus Christ, from the dead." Today the Christian community may have to say something like this: "No love is lost on this earth." Note that the latter formula is an authentic translation of the former. The Son of God (who is love) loved us to the end and died; but his love did not perish, and we express that belief by bearing witness to his resurrection. Our expression of this belief in new terms does not mean that we now claim to have a finished and perfect formula. Our new "evangelical" formula simply is a response to what we feel to be a characteristic anxiety of human beings. People proffer their love, but in the end it seems to be in vain. Many other expectations would call for very different formulations.

Finally, two points should be noted in connection with the persistent stress on Christian *witness*. First of all, we must admit that no evangelization can be effected if our words run counter to our deeds. On the other hand, however, no witness is in itself evangelization if it does not express the basic underlying foundation of our conduct as witnesses. No moral code or behavior can take the place of the "good news."

3. *Adding nothing further except at a pace that will allow the*

essential element to remain precisely that. This may well be the most surprising and unexpected point in Seumois's description of the task of evangelization, but its logic is inescapable.

For some time the early church clearly felt no temptation to add much to the essential core of the Christian message. It simply had not yet made explicit more items that could be added. Our situation twenty centuries later is quite different. During that period the church took on the physiognomy of a "universal religion," and structures, dogmas, polemics, mystical experiences, and liturgies developed freely.

Up to this point, however, Seumois's third feature corresponds with his first. Both refer to the essential core of the Christian message. But there is a difference between the two features insofar as the third presumes an interest in the essential core and then calls for something more. Exactly what is this *additional* element to be?

Our answer to this question is closely bound up with one of the fears discussed earlier: our fear that the gospel message no longer holds the attraction it once did. The implication is that the gospel is no longer the single blazing star in an otherwise dark sky. To some extent many evangelical values have been fleshed out to the point where they can and do lure people into associations and movements centered around values that are closely akin to those of the "good news." We need only cite the French Revolution, for example. Though it began in opposition to Christianity, it was waged in the name of three central gospel values: liberty, equality, and fraternity.

In the outlook of many, however, this is a mixed blessing. While it can be said that some modern-day values do seem to embody or resemble the gospel message, they also seem to strip the gospel of its force and novelty.

What is more, they also pose the danger of *deviation*. For example, any of the brief formulas that the Christian community might fashion to respond to other people's questions about the faith are formulas that are readily shared by other viewpoints that the Catholic church regards as erroneous. We might tell our listeners that "God is equally the father of all human beings." But if we let it go simply at that, we might well fear that they will hear the same thing in a Protestant setting and join that branch of Christianity. Likewise, if we simply tell our listeners that "no love is lost on earth," we might well fear that they will hear the same thing from the Communists and join their party.

How are we to forestall that danger and prevent such errors? Two approaches come to mind, but both work against the overall task of evangelization. The first approach would start out with our listeners' initial interest based on their own free choice; but it would then introduce some sort of pressure that would *provide us with time* to forestall any possible deviations. The second approach would be a bit more radical. Right at the start, when we are laying the groundwork for our evangelization, we would introduce elements designed to prevent any deviation.

Both, I noted above, work against the overall task of evangelization. This may already be clear to the reader, but I want to make sure. In a famous address to Italian jurists, Pope Pius XII concluded that tolerance of error was not only a *lesser evil* but could even be *the greater good*. Even though one had the means to prevent error, therefore, it might be better sometimes not to employ those means. Commenting on Pius XII's address, Cardinal Lercaro tried to further explain this teaching. He noted that it was not based on the commonly accepted notion of respect for the freedom of the erring person. Paradoxically enough, it was really based on *respect for the truth*—not for the truth *in itself* but for *the way in which truth reaches human beings*. Thus if we start out with the assumption that people do not err, we are not really respecting the truth.

If human beings are to really *take hold of* a truth, it is not enough to keep repeating it in parrot fashion. They must make it their own, which means they must have freedom and time to ponder it and work it out. What is more, they must have the opportunity to "experiment" with it, to apply it to their real life even if in an erroneous way. For the things we really get control over are things with which we make mistakes first and then learn to handle correctly. That is the way it is with mathematics, and that is the way it is with a Christian who develops *real personal conviction*. It should be obvious, then, that any use of pressure will impede the process of evangelization.

But what about the second approach? Perhaps it can escape this criticism. Unfortunately it cannot. Suppose, for example, we want to keep someone from falling into Protestant "errors." As soon as we have spelled out the essential core of the gospel, therefore, we add some other criterion stemming from the Christian experience in the sixteenth century. We inject some comment about the controversy over justification or devotion to Mary, for example. What have we done? By injecting these additional remarks, which may be based on real "truths," we have moved at a pace that destroys the essential core as such. Since the supplementary features are more concrete and tangible on the contemporary scene, since the gap between Catholics and Protestants is readily apparent, their differentiating features immediately take the place of the essential core of the Christian message. Our listener sees devotees of Mary rather than Christians, Catholics rather than Christians. The danger of dislocating the evangelization process by appealing to elements that are true and valid but secondary has not gone unnoticed. It is not Protestants alone who have warned against the dangers of devotion to Mary. The former President of the Latin American Episcopal Conference, Bishop Manuel Larraín, asked the Sacred Congregation for the Propagation of the Faith to alert preachers of the gospel to the danger of introducing devotion to Mary too soon. Her prerogatives could be introduced at a pace that would dislocate the core of the Christian message.

The elements of the Christian message, then, must be put in a proper hierarchy by adopting a proper "pace" or "rhythm." Only in this way can the essential core of that message retain its central place as such. But the need for proper pacing is not confined to the proclamation of the message by the Christian community. It must also show up in our *praxis* of the message, and this may be even more difficult.

Even if a Christian community is proclaiming the essential message *in words*, it is not and cannot be evangelizing if it judges historical realities in terms of criteria that do not reflect the same proper hierarchy.[2] If we prefer a project with a Christian label over one with greater liberative content that bears a different label, then we are submerging the essential in the secondary. If we prefer the undifferentiated unity of Christians bereft of liberation impact over commitments to liberation that are shared by some Christians and non-Christians, then once again we are letting secondary elements drown out the essential core of the Christian message. It is most important, therefore, that the matter of pace or rhythm be extended to praxis also.

The following point, however, may well be the most important one associated with this third feature of evangelization. If we are to be able to evangelize, we must divest ourselves of the three fears discussed in the previous chapter. We must stop fearing the freedom of our listeners because only through the exercise of their freedom can the gospel message become a truly personal conviction giving direction to their whole life. We must stop being afraid for the salvation of the majority; we must stop trying to bring them up to the logical minimum of faith as quickly as possible, so that we can dwell deeply and at length on the core faith that we now take for granted.[3] Finally, we must stop fearing that the gospel no longer has the power to attract human beings. As we have just seen, concrete experience can tell us nothing here unless and until we are willing to make the test with a gospel that is transmitted in an authentic way.

IS THERE EVANGELIZATION IN LATIN AMERICA TODAY?

Some readers might wonder why I did not illustrate the three basic features of authentic evangelization with concrete examples from Latin America, as I tended to do with other matters in the previous chapters.

The most obvious response, of course, is that in those chapters I was dealing with real-life *facts*, i.e., with the pastoral approach that is actually in use on our continent. By contrast, this chapter deals with a task that could be carried out *if* another pastoral approach were to be adopted.

Does this mean that evangelization, as the solid foundation for the whole life of the church, is not being carried out in Latin America? Yes, that is precisely what I am saying here. In stressing the existence of a vicious circle, I am suggesting that the church can use its own native resources and outside help to carry out enormous tasks, yet never get down to its basic task. Therein precisely lies the vicious circle.

But this is more than a suggestion or hypothesis, as I shall try to show in this section. My contention is that there are facts that prove this both directly, and even more importantly, indirectly. *Today, at least, Latin America is not being evangelized.*

Let us begin with some facts that *directly* illustrate the lack of evangelization. The first and most obvious is that evangelization does not exist as the *normal* task concerned with adults, even Christian adults. I am not playing with words here, as can be readily seen from this question: When do adults, even baptized adults, actually receive the "good news"?

Some might reply that they get the "good news" as children in catechetical lessons or in later religion classes at higher levels of education. But if one maintains that, one is not taking seriously any of the three elements of evangelization described in the previous section. Just consider the second element, for example. The expectations of an adult are very different from those of a child or an adolescent, and they are often decisive for a person's life. How are we to bring these expectations into contact with something that is really "good news," with something that will respond positively to those expectations? It is an outright sociological mistake to think that one can fashion "good news" for adults out of elements that were taught as compulsory lessons in earlier school days, though that might work on rare occasions.

Some might say that the evangelization of adults takes place through their participation in the Sunday liturgy, the liturgy of the Word in particular. Here again one is sadly mistaken. To begin with, no more than 10 percent of the Christian population participates in the Sunday liturgy; so between 80 and 90 percent of Latin American

Christians do not receive any evangelization this way. Moreover, everyone knows that the celebration of the Word rarely if ever is structured as a dialogue. The celebrant speaks to the people but he does not listen to them. Insofar as the topics highlighted by the celebration of the Word are concerned, the annual liturgical cycle tends to bring up themes that are meaningful and interconnected only when faith already exists and is grounded on solid "good news." They are often diffuse, and in any case they are logical consequences of faith rather than part of the groundwork for it. Even if some of them do fashion the groundwork for faith, they do so at a pace that suffocates the essential good news with a welter of other data concerning dogmas, Christian morality, and church functions and obligations.

Even less satisfactory in meeting the aforementioned requisites of an authentic evangelization are the pastoral talks that must precede the reception of certain sacraments: e.g., baptism, first communion, matrimony.

The only real exception in this panorama, which contrasts markedly with the general practice, is the catechumenate for adults in some large cities. It, however, is designed for adults who are converting to Christianity, often in connection with receiving the sacrament of matrimony. Previously the adults in question may have been nonbelievers or indifferent to religion.

All in all, however, the average adult Christians are not evangelized. It is simply *assumed* that they have received the good news and believe in it.

A second concrete indication of the lack of evangelization can be readily obtained by posing a question to Christians and then examining their responses. The question is this: Is Christianity "good news" for you? Why? The question is doubly informative. If adult Christians do not know how to answer it at all, then it is obvious not only that they have not been evangelized but also that the task of evangelization is not going on now—since they are the ones who should be able to answer that question when others ask them in their daily rounds.

When adult Christians do answer the question, we can easily interpret the sad meaning of their answers. For their answers clearly indicate that they are Christians either because they don't know what else they should be (the lowest level of response) or else because they are sure that God prescribed Christianity as a precondition for salvation, and that naturally entails priests, religious, church services, and so forth (the average level of response).[4]

What this means is that Christianity as a whole, with all its dogmas, rituals, structures, and moral obligations, has been built up on *something other than the good news of Jesus Christ*, something that is not the perennial wellspring of joy that makes the rest bearable, gives it justification and positive value, and "recapitulates" it in Paul's sense.

That is the fact of the matter. We do not want to focus our attention on it precisely because we do not want to probe too deeply into people's motivation. Yet the fact remains that millions of people can call themselves "Christians" without ever associating Christianity with the gospel—with some piece of good news that might represent a powerful stimulus to joy right here and now.

A third fact demonstrating the lack of evangelization has to do with language, specifically with our use of the term "apostolate." This would also include our use of the term "mission" when we talk about parish missions. The root meaning of the term "apostolate" is a "sending out." The apostle, as a bearer of the gospel message, is sent out to the outside world from within the bosom of the church. The root meaning, therefore, is practically synonymous with that of evangelization—or should be. But in most cases we now use it to refer to tasks that are performed within the confines of the church community itself. Seminarians go out on weekends to the "parish apostolate."[5] We hold "parish missions" to win back those who are indifferent to the practice of their religion or who have dropped out of the parish picture. This shift in the use of our terms is a clear indication that the church as a whole is failing to proclaim the gospel message to the outside world. Instead of making that decision, it has decided to stay within the warm and cozy confines of Christian unanimity.[6]

A fourth fact points to the same thing. In the church we find a terrible and widespread distaste for close contact with non-Christians. Joint sharing of human values and militant activism together are viewed with antipathy. But as I indicated earlier, evangelization is possible only if we are willing to listen to other people; and that presupposes close contact, familiarity, and shared commitments. The norms governing such things as mixed marriages and collaboration between Christians and Marxists clearly indicate that the church wishes to keep Christians away from non-Christians. In so doing, the church is turning its back on the task of evangelization.

This basic attitude is readily reflected in countless happenings every day. On one occasion, for example, Père Lebret visited Latin America and was invited to give a talk at the national university where Marxism was the dominant ideology. The Apostolic Nuncio found it curious that Lebret should go there rather than speak at the Dominican center frequented by Christians.

The fifth and final fact is that pastoral activity in Latin America as a whole simply does not recognize the existence of the non-believer. The whole thrust of its effort is divided up between pastoral work among *good* Christians and pastoral work among *bad* Christians. Even there the division of effort is unequal, and the non-Christian is eliminated altogether.[7]

The good Christians are those whose practice of morality and the sacraments is consistent enough with their faith. The bad Christians are those whose actual practice is not consistent with what they supposedly believe. Not long ago an advertisement for a correspondence course on the Bible pointed out that while invincible ignorance excused one from guilt, one could not plead invincible ignorance with regard to faith and the church because these could be found everywhere. Underlying that statement is a tacit assumption that exerts a decisive influence on pastoral activity in Latin America: that if Latin Americans claim they are not Christians and have no faith, they are really displaying *bad faith*. And no pastoral effort can counter that.

So all our pastoral effort is directed at the good Christians and the bad Christians. The former are the main object of this effort, though the latter come in for some share of attention through such activities as "parish missions" and similar drives. Yet such activities, however updated they may be, are not instruments for authentic evangelization. One need only look at their themes to realize that they *presuppose* faith on the part of the listeners and try to get them to act accordingly. What they try to do usually is to point out the disadvantages of not being consistent with the tenets of faith.

Just over ten years ago a huge mission was held in Buenos Aires. Its director called it "the greatest Christian event since the coming of Christ." Yet its whole thrust was in line with the outlook that I have just described. About two thousand Spanish-speaking priests were called in from other countries. Without any attempt to acculturate them to the problems of Argentinians living in Buenos Aires, they were sent out to preach. And what were the results? The resultant statistics showed that this enormous effort, which was reported to have cost eighteen million dollars, reached four percent of the population in Buenos Aires. The proportion of practicing Catholics in the city at that time was estimated to be around ten percent.

We have not yet even begun to consider, much less work out, a pastoral effort aimed at the vast majority of Latin Americans, a pastoral effort centered around preaching the gospel to *nonbelievers*—who may be practicing Catholics!

On an even deeper level, however, there are certain facts that indirectly illustrate the same lack of evangelization at every level of church life in Latin America.[8]

The first fact has to do with Christian dogmas, with the content of the faith. One can readily verify this point by checking with Christians—not with marginal Christians but with supposedly average Christians. Simply ask them what they would think about the idea of convening a new Ecumenical Council to alter certain dogmas and thus bring them more up to date. We might, for example, change the doctrine of three persons and one God to three gods and one person. We might make the sacraments optional instead of compulsory, and so forth.

I think one would quickly discover that Christians would be quite willing to follow the magisterium of the church in doing this, even though it might strike them as a bit curious at first. But if we were to ask them what changes that would produce in their own lives, in all likelihood they would say: "none." They would simply note the change, and that would be that.

This shows that in practice the intellectual content of the faith has no connection whatsoever with any "good news" that is decisive for real life. Orthodoxy is merely another prerequisite for obtaining salvation. Aside from that, one can live just as well or as badly with three gods and one person as with three persons and one God. If we ever did accept the essential core of the gospel message as "good news," that has been drowned in a flood of other disconnected elements that have taken on undue importance. If that is the case, there is little reason to expect that Christians themselves will be proclaimers of the gospel message in turn; for they have not been able to associate the doctrinal corpus they profess with any underlying "good news."

A second fact is closely related to the first. What is the typical relationship of the lay person with the content of faith? Some forty years ago the classic catechism by Astete (somewhat updated and revised by Vilariño) was widely used in Spain and Latin America. One typical question and answer, quoted by Unamuno, bears directly on our point here. Here is the catechism question: "In addition to the articles of faith (in the Creed), what else has God revealed to his Church?" The answer, obviously given by a layman, is this: "Don't ask me what else God has revealed to his Church besides the articles of faith because I don't know. Holy Mother Church has learned men who can answer that question." Here there follows a brief comment, for the first and only time in the catechism: "You are absolutely right in saying that it is up to learned men and the Church, not you, to provide a detailed explanation of matters of faith. It is enough for you yourself to pay heed to the articles of faith contained in the Creed."

We might paraphrase the point of these remarks as follows. To obtain salvation one must know something explicit about the faith, but in other areas it is better for the untutored laity not to discuss such matters lest they fall into error; all they have to do is sign a blank check and let the church fill it out, for it can do it better than they can. The laity, in other words, has only to subscribe completely to whatever the church believes, accepting it in the way it accepts it.

Of course some will say that such an outlook is of the past, that today the laity has a very different role in the church. But in the case of the Latin American church at least, I would say that the change is mainly on the administrative level. To some extent lay people share in the decision-making process and hold administrative offices. The hierarchy is more hedged in, as it were.

Insofar as matters of faith are concerned, if the situation has changed at all, it has changed in the direction of heightened conflict between the hierarchy and some groups of self-evangelized lay people. The fact is that wherever real evangelization has occurred in a group, however small it might be, its members have come to feel that real consistency between intellectual beliefs and practical behavior is a matter of life and death. Spurred on by the demands of the evangelization process, these lay people read and reflect much more than the priest does.

And so we find a curious situation, one that is evident throughout the continent of Latin America. What disturbs bishops most is not the laity who rebel against their authority but those who have sound and serious arguments, often theological arguments, to back up their positions on various questions. The answer given in the old catechism continues willy-nilly to be the pastoral norm, though it is clearly opposed to any authentic evangelization.

A third fact, closely related with what we have already said, has to do with a pastoral effort centered around what are called "obligatory truths." There is no doubt that certain truths or formulas are obligatory for all

Catholics, while others are left open to discussion by theologians. The hierarchy deems it pastorally prudent to emphasize the obligatory truths. As a result, the work of the theologian is often set apart from pastoral work; there is a division of labor between "pastors of souls" and "learned theologians." The implication is that pastors of souls can handle what is obligatory and have no need of theologians for their work; the latter, in turn, devote themselves to questions that are still open for discussion. In other words, pastors of souls know very well that Jesus Christ is true God and true man, and they also know this truth is essential to Christianity. In the meantime theologians can go off and debate such matters as the exact nature of Christ's real presence in the Eucharist. The implication is, of course, that much waste of time and possible divisiveness would ensue if the church's pastoral agents allowed themselves to get carried away with theological debates.

Unfortunately things are not that simple. The dogmas and truths that are obligatory are not so because they are adequate in themselves but because they serve as a solid point of departure for Christian praxis. If we look at the general nature of these "obligatory" dogmas, we will notice that they embody general truths that are not as yet related with concrete life. That Jesus Christ is true God and true man *should be* very important by virtue of the *consequences* it is meant to have in real life. Yet it is precisely when we get around to talking about consequences that we enter the realm of open-ended discussion. Without its attendant consequences the obligatory general truth is as true as a theorem of Pythagoras or Newton. The only problem is that we cannot *do pastoral work* with that kind of truth, however much we may try to; all we can do on that level is teach truths that have no relationship with any good news.

To establish such a relationship, we must involve ourselves in the effort of free and open-ended theological discussion. Latin America certainly has theologians who try to do this, but it risks losing them if they are systematically isolated from our pastoral effort on the pretext that the basic pastoral lines are already clear-cut.

There is another serious consequence of our present policy. In not a few places we do find Christian study groups and grassroots communities. The people in these groups keenly feel the impact of various serious problems, and they are tired of hearing general dogmas that solve nothing. As a result, many of them now have reached the point where they will ask the priest not to attend their meetings.[9] Or else we get a split within the church. One faction in the church is content with a pastoral effort that tries to play down problems. The other faction is secretly looking for some theological tool or support that can relate the Christian good news with the problems they find; and they are doing this secretly because this is not the official approach.

It should be obvious, then, that the split between a pastoral effort centered around obligatory truths and open-ended theological discussion is another indirect but telling sign that our pastoral policy ignores the task of evangelization in practice.

A fourth and very important indication of the present lack of evangelization on the Latin American continent is the way in which Christians arrive at socio-political judgments on historical events. Here we must emphasize the difference between two types of people.

When people truly receive the good news, with all the elements stipulated above, they structure their whole life to correspond with that news—no matter what their social extraction or native talents may be. The good news becomes the basic wellspring, not only of their attitudes but also of their value judgments on the historical scene in which they are living. The surface appearance of events does not impress them as much as the affinity of a given political or social movement to the deeper values associated with the good news.

Now what happens in the case of people who receive some dogmatic corpus but no good news? If they want to remain faithful to what they have received—whether it be because they are insecure or because they think their salvation depends on such fidelity—they, too, will try to interpret historical events; and they will be particularly concerned about events that somehow appeal to their Christianity. But their overall outlook has not been structured by any good news, and the dogmas accepted by them do not seem to have any connection with the substance of historical events. So their historical judgments will tend to be formulated on superficial grounds—e.g., on the basis of the ideological labels that are attached to various socio-political movements.

And so we commonly find that Latin American Christians, including the hierarchy, are pulled this way and that by ideological labels and shibboleths. It is common knowledge that Christians who have not been evangelized properly will be very sensitive to any appeal to "our Christian civilization of the West," for example. Indeed the shibboleth will impress them so much that they will not be capable of discerning whether the values supported by the shibboleth are truly Christian or not.

As we noted earlier, the Argentinian church did not raise any questions concerning the good or bad points of Perón's program for social reform. Neither did the Cuban church do that with respect to Fidel Castro later on. The church was only interested in knowing whether the government would be pro-Christian or Marxist and atheistic; and its judgment was dictated by that point.[10]

In Brazil people flocked into the streets to replace Goulart's government with a military dictatorship, and they did it in God's name. When an attempt was made to form some judgment about the military government, one of the more progressive bishops could not find any solid basis for a value judgment in the concrete course of events. He pleaded for calm, and time to get an interview with the new president to find out what his intentions were.

The Gospels tell us repeatedly that the Lord is not to be found everywhere people cry out his name. To discern this, however, one must have received the good news and made it part of oneself. That is precisely what is not happening now.

Paradoxically enough, therein lies the best hope for Christianity in Latin America. If the vicious circle embodied a real process of evangelization as well, there would be little reason to hope for the future. But if it turns out that there is an alternative approach and that, in fact, the whole work of evangelization remains to be done, then there is more than a little room for hope.

It should be obvious, of course, that evangelization does not make up the whole of the church's task. It was chosen here as the solid and suitable foundation for another possible pastoral approach in Latin America.

NOTES

1. See, for example, Oscar Cullmann, *La foi et le culte de l'Eglise primitive* (Neuchatel: Delachaux et Niestlé, 1963), part 2, pp. 49–87.

2. In 1971 the bishops of Chile issued a draft document entitled *Evangelio, política y socialismos* ("The Gospel, Politics, and Brands of Socialism"). See my comments on this document in "La Iglesia chilena ante el socialismo," *Marcha*, September 27, and October 4–10, 1971.

3. "It would be a sign of naiveté and impertinence, if not a serious mistake, for an apostle to rush in and upset the spiritual equilibrium that a person legitimately enjoys at a given moment, if the former has not been called to do it by God. Such an action might be motivated by the apostle's own anxiety, false theological theories, or an overly commercial notion of trafficking in souls. Such an action can only adversely affect any further apostolic work that might be called for at a later time. Thus the apostles cannot and should not propose to 'make conversions.' They should rather resolve to provide God with a needed instrument at the moment God himself chooses for evangelization" (See the anthology, *Salvación y construcción del mundo*, Gutiérrez-Segundo-Croatto-Catao-Comblin [Barcelona: Dilapsa, Nova Terra, 1968], p. 142).

4. It is interesting to note how this repeats the process that St. Paul describes with respect to the *law* in the Old Testament. First comes God's promise, then something from God to aid people in obtaining that promise. The Jews, and later on Christians, come to regard the supportive aid as a restrictive condition appended to the earlier agreement. In the case of the church, the promise is God's revealed plan to save all. See Segundo et al., *The Community Called Church*, Chap. 3, Clarification 4 (Maryknoll, New York: Orbis Books, 1973), pp. 73–77.

5. And what do they find when they get there? Here is what some priests in Brazil have to say: "The priest appears to be a man almost wholly dedicated to cultic worship. His main function seems to be to distribute the sacraments. He is there to celebrate Mass, baptize, marry people. . . . The people procure those services from him, and parochial life is organized around that scheme. It is weighed down by the problems of maintaining these roles and facilities. Every new parish is a new center of religious services. There is no respect for the stages involved in forming a new community as those are spelled out by Vatican II in *Ad Gentes*. Current efforts at renewal have gotten as far as the liturgy, of course. More time and energy and resources are invested in pastoral work surrounding the sacraments than in anything else, because they are necessities. But when will we have time for evangelization? When will we manage to get away from this ponderous parish structure? Isn't the task of evangelizing the primary task of the church in Brazil?" (in *Iglesia Latinoamericana: ¿Protesta o Profecía?* [Avellaneda, Argentina: Búsqueda, 1969], p. 187).

6. When the Holy See inquired about efforts being made to dialogue with nonbelievers, it is said that one episcopate in Latin America replied that it was so busy with believers that it had had no time to even think about those who were not believers.

7. "There is no doubt that all our recent pastoral activity has been aimed at trying to preserve what was a Christian world. It has been taken up with tasks and institutions that were alive and active sometime in the past, but that are now moribund. Its meager supply of personnel are dedicated to that traditional task, to the neglect of the vast majority of people who are alienated from the church" (Bishop José Dammert Bellido, "El derecho al servicio de la misión," *Informaciones Católicas Internacionales*, no. 239, May 7, 1965, p. 20).

8. See J.L. Segundo, "Intelecto y salvación," in the anthology *Salvación y construcción del mundo*, pp. 46–57; or in my book, *De la sociedad a la teología* (Buenos Aires: Ed. Carlos Lohlé, 1970), pp. 65–76.

9. "We do not take the real problems of life and people's spiritual needs as our starting point. We are greatly disturbed by certain conditioning factors that adversely affect priests and future priests, and that have to do with the current deficiencies in their training. For example, theological studies are not sufficiently immersed in real life. This makes it difficult for the student to develop a proper sensitivity, so that he can discern and deepen the theological values of daily life in the world. In the area of work, for example, what chance do we have to elaborate a theology of work, the mystery of work as creation, the mystery of societal redemption, and the moral exigencies of justice in underdeveloped countries? When we convene meetings of Christian communities, we almost never dialogue about life on this earth; we almost never explore human events in the light of the gospel and its spirit. Looking at the most recent episcopal meetings, we get the impression of a church that does not enter at all into day-to-day life and today's world" (*Iglesia latinoamericana*, pp. 187–88).

10. "The struggle is not exactly between Washington and Moscow. . . . If it were this, and Washington were not flanked by Christians, the battle would be considered lost. The battle is really going on between *Rome and Moscow*. . . . Moscow could win this battle sooner or later only if its opponents, *the forces of Rome and its closest allies*, were to lay down their arms—the Decalogue, the sacraments, and prayer" (Pastoral letter of Archbishop Enrique Pérez Serantes of Santiago, Cuba, dated November 13, 1960; it is cited by Leslie Dewart in *Christianity and Revolution: The Lesson of Cuba* [New York: Herder and Herder, 1963], p. 312).

VII Elements of a Different Ecclesiology

What can we conclude from everything said so far? From a pragmatic point of view, very little if anything. About all we can say is that we need not end up in a vicious circle; that there is another possible pastoral approach. And most importantly of all, we can emphasize the fact that one of the two possible approaches is covered under a cloak of silence; that it is taboo. If my comments manage to lift this cloak of silence to some extent, to open up discussion in pastoral circles, then I will have accomplished my purpose.

It is obvious that I have not provided any criterion for choosing one option over the other. My remarks may simply help people to discuss the problems that concern us with greater openness and frankness. By the same token, however, the need for criteria is not as great as might be expected, if what I have said in the preceding pages is true. I have dwelt upon the hidden motives that obscure the alternative approach, the three fears that presently plague us. In two instances we do not have to establish any objective criteria at all to decide what we shall do. In only one instance is an objective criterion needed. Let me explain.

First of all, we do not need criteria to decide whether we will or will not face up to the problems raised by the liberty and free choice of our interlocutors. Whether or not we choose to accept the freedom of the human adult as our starting point will depend on whether or not we are willing to accept the risk entailed and then reform our training programs so that pastoral workers will be able to shoulder the risk in a reasonable way.

The same holds true with respect to reliance on the power of the gospel itself. Its real power can only be measured if we are willing to implement an authentic process of evangelization, with all the elements it entails. It is a matter of plunging into real-life experience, not of working out objective criteria in advance.

But in one way or another, those two aspects of our option do converge toward another problem that does indeed call for some objective criterion. I am talking here about our *theological* fear for the salvation of the masses. When we examined that issue earlier, we saw that certain basic criteria already existed and that they stemmed from a specific theological image of the church and its function. In a word, they were rooted in a specific ecclesiology.

This, too, is an essential point, and I would wish that further light and discussion would be focused on it. To promote that end, I should simply like to present a brief treatment of a different ecclesiology that could serve as the basis for an alternative pastoral approach. I shall conclude, therefore, by presenting the basic elements of a different ecclesiology that I have treated in greater detail elsewhere.[1]

The church was established in the world to benefit the rest of humankind. The historical fact is that God established his church after humankind had existed on earth for at least two million years. This fact now becomes a *locus theologicus*. For if the church, with a minimum of demands and obligations, could ensure its members of some privileged status with respect to salvation, there would be no good reason for such a long delay in its establishment.

But suppose we assume what Vatican II expressly asks us to assume. *Gaudium et Spes* (no. 22) tells us that "the Holy Spirit, in a manner known only to God, offers to every man the possibility of being associated with this paschal mystery." It also tells us that "faith throws a new light on everything, manifests God's design for man's total vocation, and thus directs the mind to solutions which are fully human" (no. 11). It seems logical, then, that the church was sent to humanity as a whole so that with the church's help the problems posed by history might be solved more and more completely and satisfactorily. It would take a lengthy period of preparation before humanity could even formulate these problems, for it would take humanity a great deal of time to gain dominion over nature and resolve the crucial problems of basic everyday necessities.

By the same token, however, Vatican II tells us that the church does not possess ready-made solutions to these problems. Rather, it joins "with the rest of men in the search for truth" and contributes the help of faith, which "throws a new light on everything" (*Gaudium et Spes*, nos. 16 and 11). The church does not constitute any sort of privileged position, except insofar as any bearer of responsibility and training is privileged. The church receives in order to give. If one locates the privilege in the receiving and forgets its ultimate purpose, one is making a serious mistake.

What is more, this purpose of the church means that there are not two parallel histories. The human vocation is one and divine,[2] and hence the church is meant to be "a leaven" for human society (*Gaudium et Spes*, no. 40). If that is true, then those with responsibility in the church are not responsible for Christians but for all humanity. In other words, their responsibility for the Christian community does not terminate there; it obliges them to prepare the community to assume its task vis-à-vis the needs of the rest of humankind.

This has very practical and upsetting consequences. Factors and conditions that, in themselves, would seem to show favoritism to Christians do not do that at all. It seems to be to the advantage of Christians to be separated from the rest of humankind and not to be asked for more than they can give. But such an approach actually is to their disadvantage, because they will be judged by the effective implementation of their beliefs in the service of other human beings.

The universality of the church is qualitative, not quantitative. If the purpose of the church is not to proffer a privilege but to fulfill a function, then it obviously makes no sense to worry about the number of people who are part of the church. Instead we should worry about the ability of those who are members to carry out the function that the church has. The universality of the leaven in the parable does not consist in turning the whole mass of dough into leaven; it consists in communicating a certain quality to the mass that derives from itself but is not translated into any quantitative increase. With good reason the parable is very explicit on this point.

It makes no sense, then, to insist that the *ecclesia* is a church, not a sect. Some do that to advocate a quantitative universality. But the root meaning of the term "church," which may have been used by Christ himself in some form, is "convocation." There is no suggestion in the word that this "convocation" must be followed by universal adherence. The church can be the church of Christ and a sect at the same time, as indeed it was in the time of Paul (Acts 24:14). The only thing that matters greatly is that in one way or another the church does manage to carry out its function vis-à-vis the rest of humankind.

It also makes no sense to assert that the church, like every other human group, has a whole spectrum of adherents ranging from the most marginal and passive to the most active and responsible. To begin with, that is a sociological blunder. For just as there are religious and nonreligious groups of that sort, so there are other human groups that demand a very high threshold of ability and adherence. Consider a bomb-detection squad, for example. Everything depends upon how compatible the lower levels of adhesion are with the basic purpose of the group in question. And to answer this question with respect to the church, we cannot appeal to sociology or even the sociology of religion; we must look to divine revelation to find out what Christ intended to accomplish with his church.

In this connection we must point out that the demands of the gospel message with regard to church adherence set up a very high threshold. Moreover, when the gospel message does talk about the universality of salvation, there seems to be no assumption that it is due to the adherence of everyone in the world to that high threshold. So we are faced with an antinomy here. On the one hand the gospel message proclaims the universality of salvation; on the other hand it sets a high threshold of demands for those who would be part of the church. Our traditional pastoral approach solves the antinomy by getting rid of one of the poles: the high-level demands. But if we accept the antinomy, the only real explanation is that the universality of salvation is bound up with the church's function of service to the rest of humankind. Once again we come back to the image of the leaven in the mass of dough.

The church is not always the best place for salvation. As soon as one begins to talk about the high-level demands of the gospel message, one gets the painful impression that the possibility of salvation is diminished for many people. To pursue our earlier example, it is as if a mother were to be distressed by the fact that the strict qualifications would keep her son from getting into the bomb squad. In both cases people seem to sense that there is some privilege involved, forgetting completely the function, personal responsibility, and danger involved.

Vatican II tells us that membership in the church will help us before the judgment seat of God only if it is rooted in love (*Gaudium et Spes*, no. 14). Can we say that is the case with the many Christians who are looking for security in the church, or who find it easier to belong to the church than not because of the protection or pressure involved? It is incredible to see how the present pastoral approach in Latin America has minimized the danger involved in accepting rites and formulas as effective substitutes for real love. But the fact is that rites, devotions, credal formulas, and Christian unanimity are accepted and practiced as such, because authentic love would meet with great difficulty and repression if it were to undertake concrete tasks in the world.

Perhaps the Latin American church is partially aware of that fact. Perhaps that is why it is so disinclined to foster any sociological study that would concentrate on religious motivation rather than religious practice. In any case there is reason to suspect that the Latin American church is trying to substitute rites and formulas for real effective love. This suspicion should be brought out into the open. At our pastoral conferences we should discuss the danger that the church is putting obstacles in the way of people's salvation because nothing can take the place of love before the judgment seat of God.

As the reader can readily see, these three points have not been fully worked out or proved; but they obviously run directly counter to what we described in Chapter IV as the bases of our present pastoral approach.

Every pastoral official should realize that neither of the two ecclesiologies have been revealed by God or promulgated by the extraordinary magisterium of the church. Hence theologians and pastors of souls are free to discuss them as they wish. But two courses are indeed out of the question. First, we could use a pastoral approach that straddles the fence and tries to borrow elements from each of the two alternative ecclesiologies. The two ecclesiologies are contradictory, so some choice between them must be made on the basis of principle. Second, we cannot silence discussion and debate by appealing to shibboleths. We cannot blandly accuse dissenters of "elitism" or evade decisions by appealing to the "church of the poor." We must face up to our problems and discuss them in clear-eyed terms, in accordance with the most sound and most venerable traditions of pastoral theology.

NOTES

1. See Segundo et al., *The Community Called Church*, Eng. trans. (Maryknoll, New York: Orbis Books, 1973).

2. "All construction of the future that involves human reason and creative intelligence, every effort to make sure that this future will get beyond bondage to nature insofar as that is possible, not to mention the increasing 'socialization' of human existence that proposes to grant the maximum of freedom to each individual—all of this, in the eyes of Christianity, represents a task inscribed in human nature itself as willed by God. It is an obligation that forms an integral part of a properly religious outlook. And this outlook in turn, is simply human liberty opening up in faith and hope to the absolute future" (Karl Rahner, "El porvenir cristiano del hombre," *Informaciones Católicas Internacionales*, no. 242, June 22, 1965, p. 26).

OTHER ORBIS TITLES

THE COMING OF THE THIRD CHURCH
An Analysis of the Present and Future of the Church

Walbert Buhlmann

"*Not a systematic treatment of contemporary ecclesiology but a popular narrative analogous to Alvin Toffler's Future Shock.*" America

ISBN 0-88344-069-5 CIP *Cloth $12.95*
ISBN 0-88344-070-9 *Paper $6.95*

FREEDOM MADE FLESH

Ignacio Ellacuría

"*Ellacuría's main thesis is that God's saving message and revelation are historical, that is, that the proclamation of the gospel message must possess the same historical character that revelation and salvation history do and that, for this reason, it must be carried out in history and in a historical way.*" Cross and Crown

ISBN 0-88344-140-3 *Cloth $8.95*
ISBN 0-88344-141-1 *Paper $4.95*

CHRISTIAN POLITICAL THEOLOGY
A MARXIAN GUIDE

Joseph Petulla

"*Petulla presents a fresh look at Marxian thought for the benefit of Catholic theologians in the light of the interest in this subject which was spurred by Vatican II, which saw the need for new relationships with men of all political positions.*" Journal of Economic Literature

ISBN 0-88344-060-1 *Paper $4.95*

THE GOSPEL IN SOLENTINAME
Ernesto Cardenal

"Upon reading this book, I want to do so many things—burn all my other books which at best seem like hay, soggy with mildew. I now know who (not what) is the church and how to celebrate church in the eucharist. The dialogues are intense, profound, radical. The Gospel in Solentiname calls us home." Carroll Stuhlmueller, National Catholic Reporter

ISBN 0-88344-168-3 CIP　　　　　　　　　　　　　　　　　　　Cloth $6.95

THE CHURCH AND POWER IN BRAZIL
Charles Antoine

"This is a book which should serve as a basis of discussion and further study by all who are interested in the relationship of the Church to contemporary governments, and all who believe that the Church has a vital role to play in the quest for social justice." Worldmission

ISBN 0-88344-062-8　　　　　　　　　　　　　　　　　　　　Paper $4.95

HISTORY AND THE THEOLOGY OF LIBERATION
Enrique Dussel

"The book is easy reading. It is a brilliant study of what may well be or should be the future course of theological methodology." Religious Media Today

ISBN 0-88344-179-9　　　　　　　　　　　　　　　　　　　　Cloth $8.95
ISBN 0-88344-180-2　　　　　　　　　　　　　　　　　　　　Paper $4.95

LOVE AND STRUGGLE IN MAO'S THOUGHT
Raymond L. Whitehead

"Mao's thoughts have forced Whitehead to reassess his own philosophy and to find himself more fully as a Christian. His well documented and meticulously expounded philosophy of Mao's love and struggle-thought might do as much for many a searching reader." Prairie Messenger

ISBN 0-88344-289-2 CIP　　　　　　　　　　　　　　　　　　Cloth $8.95
ISBN 0-88344-290-6　　　　　　　　　　　　　　　　　　　　Paper $3.95

A THEOLOGY OF LIBERATION
Gustavo Gutiérrez

"*The movement's most influential text.*" Time

ISBN 0-88344-477-1   *Cloth $7.95*
ISBN 0-88344-478-X   *Paper $4.95*

THE NEW CREATION: MARXIST AND CHRISTIAN?
José María González-Ruiz

"*A worthy book for lively discussion.*" The New Review of Books and Religion

ISBN 0-88344-327-9 CIP   *Cloth $6.95*

CHRISTIANS AND SOCIALISM
Documentation of the Christians for Socialism Movement in Latin America

edited by John Eagleson

"*Compelling in its clear presentation of the issue of Christian commitment in a revolutionary world.*" The Review of Books and Religion

ISBN 0-88344-058-X   *Paper $4.95*

POLYGAMY RECONSIDERED
Eugene Hillman

"*This is by all odds the most careful consideration of polygamy and the attitude of Christian Churches toward it which it has been my privilege to see.*" Missiology

ISBN 0-88344-391-0   *Cloth $15.00*
ISBN 0-88344-392-9   *Paper $7.95*

AFRICAN TRADITIONAL RELIGION
E. Bolaji Idowu

"*A great work in the field and closely comparable to Mbiti's African Religions and Philosophy. It is worthwhile reading.*" The Jurist

ISBN 0-88344-005-9   *Cloth $6.95*

CHRISTIANS, POLITICS AND VIOLENT REVOLUTION

J.G. Davies

"Davies argues that violence and revolution are on the agenda the world presents to the Church and that consequently the Church must reflect on such problems. This is a first-rate presentation, with Davies examining the question from every conceivable angle." National Catholic News Service

ISBN 0-88344-061-X *Paper $4.95*

THEOLOGY FOR A NOMAD CHURCH

Hugo Assmann

"A new challenge to contemporary theology which attempts to show that the theology of liberation is not just a fad, but a new political dimension which touches every aspect of Christian existence." Publishers Weekly

ISBN 0-88344-493-3 *Cloth $7.95*
ISBN 0-88344-494-1 *Paper $4.95*

ASIAN VOICES IN CHRISTIAN THEOLOGY

Edited by Gerald H. Anderson

"A basic sourcebook for anyone interested in the state of Protestant theology in Asia today. I am aware of no other book in English that treats this matter more completely." National Catholic Reporter

ISBN 0-88344-017-2 *Cloth $15.00*
ISBN 0-88344-016-4 *Paper $7.95*

THE PRAYERS OF AFRICAN RELIGION

John S. Mbiti

"We owe a debt of gratitude to Mbiti for this excellent anthology which so well illuminates African traditional religious life and illustrates so beautifully man as the one who prays." Sisters Today

ISBN 0-88344-394-5 CIP *Cloth $7.95*

AFRICAN CULTURE AND THE CHRISTIAN CHURCH

Aylward Shorter

"*An introduction to social and pastoral anthropology, written in Africa for the African Christian Churches.*" Western Catholic Reporter

ISBN 0-88344-004-0   *Paper $6.50*

WATERBUFFALO THEOLOGY

Kosuke Koyama

"*This book with its vivid metaphors, fresh imagination and creative symbolism is a 'must' for anyone desiring to gain a glimpse into the Asian mind.*" *Evangelical Missions Quarterly*

ISBN 0-88344-702-9   *Paper $4.95*

THE CHURCH AND THIRD WORLD REVOLUTION

Pierre Bigo

"*Heavily documented, provocative yet reasonable, this is a testament, demanding but impressive.*" Publishers Weekly

ISBN 0-88344-071-7 CIP   *Cloth $8.95*
ISBN 0-88344-072-5   *Paper $4.95*

If your bookdealer is sold out, please send your order to Dept. BB, Orbis Books, Maryknoll, New York 10545. Please order by number and title. Complete catalog of 116 titles available on request.